"Ayers highlights the enormous cost of employee disengagement, addresses the root causes, and shows ways to create an environment built on trust that recaptures employees' enthusiasm and ignites their passion to perform. He shows trust is the foundation of successful relationships and that organizations cannot achieve and sustain high-performance without high levels of trust. His observations on trust, ways to increase it, and benefits from it are solid and fully consistent with my research on high performing teams."

Dr Raymond Vlasin, Distinguished Professor Emeritus,
Michigan State University, Co-Author of
Increasing the Odds for High-performance Teams

"You may be used to measuring your bottom line in terms of dollars and cents, but what Keith talks about in this book helped us learn to how to measure our bottom line in how we change the lives of those that we serve. Now I can appreciate where we were, the process we went through, and the fact that we're doing these initiatives to serve families and make a difference. That's the bottom line. By applying the principals in this book our agency is changing lives for the right reasons and in the right ways."

Susan Osborne, Director, Department of Social Services,
Alamance County, NC

"One of my favorite phrases is 'managers manage things and leaders develop people.' This book couldn't do a better job re-iterating this sentiment and explaining in practical terms how it will improve anyone's leadership style. Keith is an expert on group dynamics. He understands and outlines all of the different personality traits and leadership styles, and gives instruction on how to create productive, high-energy teams using emotional intelligence. But most importantly, Keith teaches everybody how empowerment and a dedicated resolve to knowing and developing your people makes a difference in both your office environment and the quality of your employees' work."

Ken Wright, President, TheWrightCoach.com
Former General Manager, Westpac Financial Services (Australia)

"Realize it. Embrace it. What Keith says so eloquently in this book completely changed the way I saw myself as a leader. These ideas helped me transform my company's culture, and they can help you transform yours too."

Carol A. Scott, President/COO AAA of South Jersey

"Keith uses personal anecdotes and real-life examples to capture the essence of what it takes to create a great workplace. By implementing these ideas, Unity Health Center has significantly improved our employee retention. Leadership has changed. People trust one another, and they enjoy coming to work. Everyone in healthcare should read this book."

Linda Brown, Vice President, Clinical & Support Services,
Unity Health Center

"Whether you run a hospital or a manufacturing company, your directors and employees must be actively engaged and working as partners if you want accomplish your mission. Keith's book will guide you step by step through the process of creating that partnership."

Chuck Skillings, President/CEO, Unity Health Center

"In this thought-provoking book, Ayers proves that for an organization to be successful, it must be built on a foundation of trust. Leaders who are mentors and team motivators win. His emphasis on shared leadership is consistent with my own research, where none of the high performing teams I analyzed reported directly to a command-and-control leader. CEOs take note: not only does this book reveal the secret to sustained success, it shows you how to realize your dream."

Dr Arlen Leholm, Executive Director, North Central Regional Association (NCRA), Co-Author of *Increasing the Odds for High Performance Teams*

ENGAGEMENT IS NOT ENOUGH

ENGAGEMENT
IS NOT
ENOUGH

You Need Passionate Employees
To Achieve Your Dream

Keith E. Ayers

Published by Elevate, Charleston, South Carolina.
Member of Advantage Media Group.

ELEVATE is a registered trademark and the
Advantage colophon is a trademark of Advantage Media Group, Inc.

Printed in the United States of America
ISBN: 978-1-60194-023-0

We would like to acknowledge Inscape Publishing, Inc. for permission to reprint the following material.

- *DiSC. Classic* © Copyright 2001 by Inscape Publishing, Inc. All rights reserved. Used by permission of Inscape Publishing, Inc. "DiSC" is a registered trademark of Inscape Publishing, Inc.
- *Work Expectations Profile* © Copyright 2001 by Inscape Publishing, Inc. All rights reserved. Used by permission of Inscape Publishing, Inc.
- *Personal Listening Profile .* © Copyright 1995 by Inscape Publishing, Inc. All rights reserved. Used by permission of Inscape Publishing, Inc. "Personal Listening Profile" is a registered trademark of Inscape Publishing, Inc.
- *Discovering Diversity Profile.* © Copyright 1994 by Inscape Publishing, Inc. All rights reserved. Used by permission of Inscape Publishing, Inc. "Discovering Diversity Profile" is a registered trademark of Inscape Publishing, Inc.
- *Team Dimensions Profile* © Copyright 1995 by Inscape Publishing, Inc. All rights reserved. Used by permission of Inscape Publishing, Inc.
- *DiSC. Indra.* © Copyright 2003 by Inscape Publishing, Inc. All rights reserved. Used by permission of Inscape Publishing, Inc. "DiSC" and "Indra" are registered trademarks of Inscape Publishing, Inc.

Library of Congress Cataloging-in-Publication Data
Ayers, Keith E.
  Engagement is not enough! : you need passionate employees to achieve your dream / by Keith E. Ayers.
    p. cm.
  ISBN 978-1-60194-023-0
  1. Employee motivation. 2. Personnel management. 3. Leadership. I. Title.
  HF5549.5.M63A94 2008
  658.3'14--dc22

                                                2008007680

This book is dedicated to
My parents Bernard and Catherine Ayers
Whose commitment and passion for their life work as Salvation Army missionaries helped shape my values and beliefs and taught me the meaning of the word courage.

My wife Kelley
Whose love and support make my life more meaningful and give me the opportunity to pursue my passion for making the world of work a place where people want to and can be their best.

My children Bradley, Martin, Lauren, and Melissa
All of whom had the courage to pursue their passions, and who have taught me countless lessons in the process.

TABLE OF CONTENTS

FOREWORD

By Curt W. Coffman, Co-Author, *First, Break All the Rules, What the World's Greatest Managers Do Differently* (Simon & Schuster) and *Follow this Path*, (Warner Books) and Chief Science Officer for the MAJERS Corporation.

Engagement has become a very popular term, portraying all things related to business, from employee to customer and even shareholder. New metaphors are important as they help us transition, shedding old mental models and slipping into new ways of thinking. The problem with new language is that while it quickly generates common understanding, it tends to be soon misapplied. This misapplication prevents us from expanded learning. I once had a college professor who drew a circle on the blackboard and stated that the volume of the circle quantified what we know. He then declared that the circumference of the circle measured what we do not know. As the volume increases, so does the circumference.

Keith Ayers possesses an unending curiosity combined with a compelling need to make sense of challenging issues. His natural ability to observe—and then frame a concern with a practical understanding that leads to a solution—is a rare gift. While it is not always easy to stand eye-to-eye with tough and seemingly unsolvable challenges, he finds it energizing and motivating. Across the pages of this book, you will experience that "oomph" and true understanding of the human condition.

As you will see throughout this book, Keith has courageously expanded prior learning and, consequently, shown what needs to be unlearned. The importance of people's engagement within an organization is something no one debates. The problem organizations face today is how to insure the right leadership, strategy, and culture are in place to create and sustain engagement.

Engagement Is Not Enough provides a refreshing approach, not only to understanding the people side of enterprise, but also to how you can embrace it. Its broad attention, from the most basic human needs to the new demands of leadership, is both practical and immediately useful. Theory is good, but if that's what you want, buy a different book. This book is about real change and application.

Keith's position that passion is the outcome of involvement, attachment, and trust is proven through research and application. This position challenges you to examine the question: is true excellence possible without a deep sense of purpose and passion for what you do every day?

ACKNOWLEDGEMENTS

The starting point for the ideas in this book was Ron Bates and Ralph Colby starting Integro, a two-man consulting company, in February 1973. The idea that trust was essential for personal and organizational success was not new, but the model Ralph developed, the **Elements of Trust**™, redefined the behaviors required to build trust into simple, practical guidelines in a way no one else has managed to do before or since. Thank you Ron and Ralph for creating this wonderful organization and for your inspirational leadership, friendship, and personal guidance, especially through my early years with Integro.

David McNally, author of *Even Eagles Need a Push*, deserves a special thank you for bringing Integro to Australia, and for giving me a *push* when I doubted my own ability. You'll read more about how that happened in Chapter 1.

I am grateful to all of the clients who have placed their trust in Integro over the past twenty-nine years. Your enthusiasm for creating a work environment based on trust and personal responsibility and your commitment to personally applying the principles have allowed me to continue to learn and grow from your experience.

In addition, I would like to thank the incredibly talented team of people at Inscape Publishing Inc., who have produced such a valuable suite of learning instruments that have enabled our clients to move to levels of achievement they could not have reached without the emotional intelligence these tools helped them develop. Inscape's ongoing research and creativity has had a significant impact on Integro's success.

I am privileged to have had the support of many other independent consultants who have taken the materials we have developed and successfully used them with their own clients. To all of our associates, thank you for believing in us and for the effort you have put into helping organizations create a more successful workplace.

A special thank you to Paige Stover Hague and her team at The Ictus Initiative, in particular Carolyn McKibbin and Ben Berzai, without whose help this book would not be complete. And to Ann McIndoo, who created the book writer's bootcamp that got the book out of my head and onto paper.

I would like to give special thanks to Jeff and Rosanne Taylor from RC Taylor and Associates in West Chester, Pennsylvania for welcoming us into their family when we moved to the United States in August 2001. We met through business, became friends, and it was their belief in our work and encouragement to expand our business into the US that made it possible for us to make the move.

I am particularly indebted to the team at Integro Learning Company in Australia, who supported me through thick and thin, and without whom Integro would not be the successful organization it is today. David Flint, our General Manager, took over the reins of the Australian operation, allowing me to fulfill my dream of taking our business to North America. I could not have done that without such a capable, trustworthy person as David. Frank Cahill, Michael Neaves, and Brad Jobe, our full-time consultants, are as talented a group of people as I have ever had the opportunity to work with. Their passion for our work and ability to work together as a team have taken our company to new levels. Alf Horan, Geri Phil, and Jackie Cormie do a wonderful job of ensuring that our clients are delighted with every aspect of their relationship with Integro.

Finally, I am extremely grateful for my good fortune to be married to Kelley. Not only has she been my life partner for twenty years and a wonderful mother to our daughter Melissa, she is also my business partner, having worked full-time in our business for most of those years. Integro's successful expansion into the United States is primarily due to Kelley's commitment to excellence and the quality support she provides our clients and associates. Although Kelley is willing to take risks, including relocating to the United States in 2001, she adds an important balance in my life by keeping my feet on the ground with her down-to-earth reminders about day-to-day realities. It takes a very special person to put up with my foibles both at work and at home.

INTRODUCTION

If I asked you to tell me the most serious threat to the health of your business, what would you say? Increased competition, perhaps? The threat of emerging markets overseas? The state of the economy? I will tell you now that the most serious threat to the health of your business is not an external phenomenon—it lurks within your organization: *employee disengagement*. The threat is real and the effects could be terminal. Fighting *employee disengagement* must be taken seriously by every leader in your organization. It is a leadership issue. The Gallup Organization has performed ongoing research on *employee engagement* for over a decade now and has identified three types of employees: *Engaged, Not Engaged,* and *Actively Disengaged*. In their book **Follow This Path**, Curt Coffman and Gabriel Gonzalez-Molina, Ph.D. report the average employee engagement figures for the United States: 30 percent *Engaged*, 54 percent *Not Engaged*, and 16 percent *Actively Disengaged*.[1]

The problem is very real. The numbers don't lie. One of the least obvious but most significant costs of *employee disengagement* is the percentage of payroll that is wasted on *disengaged* employees.

In organizations with only average levels of *employee engagement*, between 30 and 50 percent of their payroll is going down the drain. You pay out 100 percent of payroll and benefits to all employees, but those who are *not engaged* give you 50 percent or less of what you pay them for... which is to give you their best performance. The *not engaged* and, to a larger degree, the *actively disengaged* employees are very costly, taking their pay and benefits and then working against the best interests of your organization. They spread their discontent and do their best to turn the *engaged* employees against you as well. Even if they don't succeed, they will undermine the good work your *engaged* employees are doing by failing to complete their part of projects on time or lowering the overall quality of the job.

Why Are So Few Employees Engaged?

When employees join your organization, they start out as engaged and ready to take responsibility. They applied for the job because it interested them, and they believed they had the talents, skills, and creativity that the job required. So did you, which is why you hired them. On day one, they are excited about getting the job, switched on, and ready to make a contribution to your organization. So what happens to bring the average engagement level down to 30 percent?

An employee's first six months with your organization are critical. Coffman and Gonzalez-Molina say that "on average, in the first six months of employment, 38 percent of employees are engaged…after ten years of employment, the proportion of the engaged drops to 20 percent."[2]

Think about that. During the first six months, an average of over 60 percent of employees switch off, then engagement continues to decline over time. This is not just an American problem. Engagement in industrialized and developed nations like Canada, Germany, Japan, the United Kingdom, and Australia are at or below the numbers posted in the United States, proving this problem to be a global one.

The Switching Off Process

What happens during that first six months? New employees start with high expectations and enthusiasm, believing, *"This is the job for me!"* After all, it was a big decision to accept the job. The decline starts when they realize that their expectations are not being met, and they begin to wonder, *"Did I make a mistake?"* They start talking with their co-workers about their expectations only to get confirmation that their expectations are not going to be met. Because they are new to the company, they are apprehensive about speaking up. Finally, in a last ditch effort, they talk with their manager to see if they can improve things and get some of their expectations met. But nothing changes; the employees realize the situation is not going to change. They give up on getting their expectations met, *switch off*, and start thinking about leaving. The final stage is when they decide to quit and actively begin to look for another job, or, more commonly and costly, *they quit and stay!* ↓ *Because in order to tolerate, we have to disconnect.*

Leadership Has Failed!

For such a high percentage of employees to become *disengaged* over the first six months, there must be a significant failure at the leadership level. Leaders at all levels have not sustained the natural enthusiasm and commitment their employees had when they started with the organization. Despite the billions of dollars spent on leadership development every year and the thousands of resources on the subject, the primary objective of effective leadership, getting all employees to perform at their best, is not being achieved. Even with the increased focus put on *employee engagement* over the past ten years, the percentage of *engaged* employees overall has increased by barely one or two percent.

Why?

Many leaders do not even recognize the threat to the health of their organization, so they do nothing to treat it. Many of those managers aware of the problem look for a quick fix, attempting to cure it with a stop-gap measure. They throw money at the problem, thinking that better compensation, benefits, incentives, or working conditions will fix it. If a raise has any impact on *engagement* at all, then it only lasts one or two months, tops. *Just as there is no quick fix to any relationship.*

The truth is, there is no quick fix for the problem of *disengagement.* If you are serious about getting your employees to be as *passionate* about your dream for your organization as you are—which is most likely why you are reading this book—focus on igniting the *passion* in your employees, not on getting them *engaged. Passionate* employees are *engaged,* and then some. There is no confusion about *passion*—you can't buy it with money. That is the reason this book is titled *Engagement Is Not Enough!* To get the best out of everyone on your team, you need to aim high.

Getting your team to be as *passionate* as you are about your vision and goals will take time and exceptional leadership. It requires a commitment from you to provide the leadership that gets people *engaged* and then develops them into a *high-performance team.* This book will guide you through the steps to achieving that, but first, I ask you to think seriously about what is really important to you. Do you really want to create a great organization, one that not only achieves outstanding results, but that also attracts and retains the most talented people in your field?

If you do, then first make sure that you are not consumed by one of the four primary obsessions that result in managers unintentionally increasing the threat of *disengagement.* These are:

- **An obsession with financial results.** Financial success is critical to any organization. But to drive myopically toward profit or meeting budget alone, ignoring the needs of employees, customers, and the culture and values of the organization, is very costly to results. Being obsessed with the bottom line can achieve good results, but think how much more you could achieve with *passionate* employees who go to extreme lengths every day to give their best performance? Lasting success comes from employees who are switched on and *passionately* supporting your organization. You invest in them and they, in turn, invest in you.

- **An obsession with control**. *Control-based* leaders assume that people cannot be trusted, and they send that message to their teams. They micromanage employees, believing that tasks will not be completed to their standards unless they are checking on their teams. They assume employees do not really want to work, and therefore they need to continue to drive them to achieve results. They also believe that, as the manager, they have all the knowledge and experience, and therefore they need to make all the decisions about how to improve performance. There is no research that shows this approach achieves superior results; in fact, the opposite is true. These autocrats are a liability to the organization, squashing natural enthusiasm, creativity, and ambition and driving away the most talented employees.

- **An obsession with avoiding responsibility.** Lack of engagement, performance problems, and high levels of employee turnover—it is never the fault of the leaders. They blame their employees or other external factors, when what they really should be doing is looking in the mirror! The number one cause of lack of engagement, poor employee performance, and staff turnover is the relationship the employee has with his or her immediate supervisor. In another book from The Gallup Organization, ***Now, Discover Your Strengths,*** authors Marcus Buckingham and Donald O. Clifton say, "…The single most important determinant of individual performance is a person's relationship with his or her immediate manager. Without a robust relationship with a manager who sets clear expectations, knows you, trusts you, and invests in you, you are less likely to stay and perform."[3] If your team is not performing the way you want them to, first look at whether the leadership they are getting from you is what they need in order to be able to perform at their best.

- **An obsession with logic.** The left-brain is the rational, analytical, logical, sequentially-thinking side of the brain. The world of work has been ruled by left-brained thinking since the beginning of the Industrial Age. The executive offices of most organizations are dominated by left-brained professionals such as engineers, accountants, economists, lawyers, scientists, and businesspeople. Yet every organization, whether its leaders realize it or not, is in the people business! You hire people, sell or provide services to people, and partner with people. Well, people have feelings. Managers obsessed with *logic* and left-brained thinking are dismissive of feelings—they say that emotions don't belong in the workplace. They do not believe *engagement* has anything to do with organizational performance or that people can be *passionate* about their work. *"They just need to do their jobs,"* they say, as they switch off any *en-*

gagement their employees have. Managers need to understand that emotional intelligence and right-brain thinking are critical skills for becoming successful leaders in the new global economy.

What's the Solution?

When I asked this question of a Tampa-based senior executive team a couple of years ago, one of them said, "That's easy. We just need to identify who the disengaged people are and get rid of them. Then we can hire just engaged people." What he had forgotten was that they had already hired predominately *engaged* people. If they did not change their *leadership approach*, and therefore the work environment, this new crop of *engaged* workers would soon become *disengaged*. It is a never-ending cycle that cannot be defeated until new ideas come into play about how to lead an effective team whose members are not only *engaged* in their work, but also emotionally invested in what they are doing for your organization.

By now you may be thinking, *"Don't the employees have a responsibility to be engaged and perform at their best?"* And you're right, they do. They <u>should</u> be *engaged*. But the reality is, in an average organization, 70 percent of them are not! Being *right* about what they should do won't make them more *engaged*. Being *effective* as a leader will. The leadership required to light a fire within people, rather than under them, starts at the top of an organization's hierarchy, moves down through middle management, progresses on to the frontline workers, and turns customers into advocates who actively promote your organization. It's a domino effect. Being switched on is contagious, but so is being switched off. Until you inspire that *passion*, nothing will change.

That you picked up this book reassures me of your commitment to combating the problem of *employee disengagement*. It also means that you have a dream for your organization, and that you know you cannot achieve it without the support of a *passionate* group of people. This book addresses the root causes of *employee disengagement* and puts you on the path to not only recapturing the enthusiasm and optimism your employees had on their first day with you, but also to creating an environment that will ignite their *passion* to perform at their very best.

Why Leadership Training Hasn't Worked

For almost thirty years, I have been working as a consultant with leaders from hundreds of organizations in many different countries. As a result of this experience, our organization, Integro Leadership Institute LLC, has developed a process-driven approach to creating *high-performance* organizations. Our experience is that the traditional approach used to develop the skills that leaders need to increase *engagement* is fundamentally flawed. Millions of dollars a year are wasted on leadership training that has no impact on the organization's culture or the level of *employee engagement.*

There are three primary reasons leadership training fails to achieve business results:

- **Most leadership training is an event.** Whether it is two days, five days, or three weeks, if leadership training is a one-time event, then its impact on organizational behavior will be negligible. In the best-selling book ***Primal Leadership,*** authors Daniel Goleman, Richard Boyatzis, and Annie McKee say, "The thinking brain can comprehend something after a single hearing or reading. The limbic brain, on the other hand, is a much slower learner—particularly when the challenge is to relearn deeply ingrained habits. The difference matters immensely when trying to improve leadership skills."[4] A leadership development event will not turn you into an exceptional leader. To achieve that requires the development of many skills, repetition, and consistent application over a period of time.

- **Most leadership training does not develop emotional intelligence.** Again, because most training is event-based, your knowledge of *emotional intelligence* is limited to what you can glean from a single sitting. It takes time, repetition, and consistent application for managers to overcome their fear of losing control enough to trust people and allow them to work without supervision. You have not developed *emotional intelligence* until you have learned to manage your emotions and behave in a way that brings out the best in everyone.

- **There is no accountability.** Most leadership development initiatives do not require leaders to be *accountable* for applying what they have learned. In most cases, it is entirely up to the individuals to decide how much of what they have learned they will apply. Far too often, the application is zero; they slip back into their old habits and nothing changes.

This book will take you through the steps in the process we use to successfully create a *high-performance* workplace. You will have the opportunity to take time out at each step and apply what you are learning, but the commitment to do that is up to you.

Trust Is Essential

When Ron Bates and Ralph Colby founded Integro in Minneapolis, Minnesota in February of 1973, they understood that management development—we did not talk much about leadership back then—was focused on developing task skills rather than people skills. Though the notion of "engagement" had not really come into vogue, our founders recognized that *trust* is the foundation of all successful relationships, and that organizations could not achieve their potential without a consistently high *level of trust* with their employees and customers.

As a result of extensive research, Ralph identified the **Elements of Trust**™— four basic ingredients which must be present in a relationship for *trust* to develop. This simple, powerful concept is the foundation of all the work that Integro Leadership Institute does with clients, and because it is so important, I have devoted the whole of Chapter 3 to this model. It applies to managers at all levels, salespeople, and customer service staff; everyone in your organization who works with people needs to know how to *build trust*.

Early on, Ron and Ralph realized they were on to something when consultants from overseas started contacting them wanting to represent Integro, without any real promotion from our end. In the space of just three years, we expanded into nine countries, then three years later into nineteen countries, all by word of mouth. Our *trust model*, the **Elements of Trust**™, was the primary catalyst for our growth. There was not anything on the market at the time that directly addressed *trust* with such a simple, practical approach as Integro did and, to my knowledge, that's still the case.

I joined Integro in May of 1977, was trained by Ron and Ralph in the United States, and then returned to Australia to work for Integro. For the next few years, I operated mainly in Australia and New Zealand. My first real international consulting experience was in the Philippines in 1984, working with a group of Price Waterhouse partners from seven different countries throughout Southeast Asia. I also spent some time in Hong Kong and Shanghai working with multinational clients.

In working with so many different cultures, I've found that **Elements of Trust**™ and the values behind them apply effectively to all cultures. Cultural differences do need to be taken into account in their application, however. For example, saving face is very important in most Asian cultures; it is in very bad taste to say something that makes another person look bad or hurts his or her feelings. So while straightforwardness is important in clarifying expectations and *building trust*, it must be done with more care and sensitivity with people from those cultures. It wouldn't hurt to apply that in all cultures!

What Is Leadership?

Because there are so many divergent views on what leadership is, and this book is about leadership, I want to elaborate here on the approach that produces the best results according to our research. Too much of what has been written about leadership has leaders focusing on themselves. It's the self-focused leaders that switch people off. The *What's in it for me* approach is not as successful as the approach *What's in it for my organization* or *What's in it for us*. Jim Collins expresses it well in the book ***Good to Great*** with his description of the Level 5 leader: "Level 5 leaders blend the paradoxical combination of deep personal humility with intense professional will. This rare combination also defies our assumptions about what makes a great leader."[5] Collins' research found that Level 5 leadership is a requirement for achieving greatness.

Leadership Is an Act, Not a Role!

You are seen to be a leader only when you perform an *act of leadership*. It is a behavior and approach to management. The three stages to an *act of leadership* are *Out, In,* and then *Out* again:

1. You see something *Out* there that needs changing, fixing, or improving.
2. You go *In* to process your thoughts, feelings, and observations and make choices about what can be done to change, fix, or improve what you have noticed.
3. Finally, you act *Out* your decision to change, fix, or improve it.

Anyone can perform an *act of leadership*. Take Mary, a data entry operator. Mary's job is to take forms customers send in and type the details into a software program. The problem is the data goes into the software in a different sequence than it is collected on the form. This makes it more time-consuming for the staff to enter the data. Typically, what happens in a situation like this is that employees talk amongst each other and say things like, "Wouldn't you think they would do something about this?" Too often this is where the conversation ends. But not for Mary!

Mary thinks about the situation for awhile with the aim to redesign the form so that the data can be entered more efficiently. She experiments with new designs that could save her minutes on each form she processes, minutes which, over time, add up. And she is just one data processor, so if her plan were implemented, it would save her team and her company many hours and lots of money. She takes this idea to her supervisor because she hasn't the authority to change the form herself. Perhaps Mary's supervisor doesn't either. But Mary acts on it.

Mary saw something (*Out*) that needed to be changed, so she thought about (*In*) how she could solve the problem. Then, Mary completed her *act of leadership* by taking action (*Out* again) to redesign the form, which is as far as she could take this step without approval from a supervisor. The supervisor's role here was to support Mary's *act of leadership*. Unfortunately, some supervisors will say, "Mary, we don't have the authority to change the form." But not Mary's supervisor! She supported Mary's *act of leadership* and the redesigned form was implemented.

Wouldn't you like everyone on your team to speak up when he or she sees things that could improve productivity, reduce costs, and increase customer satisfaction? That is the outcome of *shared leadership*—when everyone on the team takes responsibility for speaking up and performing acts of leadership.

Leaders and Followers

When the word "leader" is used, the word "follower" is usually not far behind. You may have noticed that I've been using the term "supporting" rather than "following." This is an important distinction for you as a leader. If you see people as followers, you expect them to follow. More importantly, if they view themselves as followers, then that is just how they'll act. Some leaders prefer this drone mentality, but those leaders cannot expect employees to speak up when they see things that need to be changed, fixed, or improved.

when I support you, I am going to offer helpful feedback, if I am a follower, I will do just that.

You cannot complete an *act of leadership* without the support of others. No support, no leadership! The only power you really have as a leader is that granted to you by those who support you. It is the supporters who have the power to make things happen—or not happen, as the case may be. When everyone on your team is *passionate* and looking for opportunities to contribute *acts of leadership*, the power that will be unleashed will achieve results way beyond what you could ever achieve by any other means.

Gaining Others' Support

Turning a group of employees with varying levels of *engagement* into a *high-performance team* won't happen overnight. It takes time, commitment, patience, and the belief that the effort is worth it. Why do most leaders fail to create *high-performance teams*? Because they are not willing to do what has to be done! Unfortunately, as I've said earlier, there is no shortcut. But there are ways to switch your team on over time.

they disengage – they disconnect

If employees' needs are not met, they switch off and eventually look for somewhere else to work. It's no different than you looking for a new computer supplier if your existing brand does not satisfy your needs. There are five primary needs employees have that <u>must</u> be met if they are to become *passionate* about their work and your organization. They form a hierarchy, meaning that you have to start at level one. The lower-level needs must be met and continue to be satisfied before they will look to you, their leader, to satisfy the higher-level needs.

The Passion Pyramid™

Need to be on a Winning Team

Need for Meaning

Need to be an "Insider"

Need to Learn and Grow

Need for Respect

Employee Needs

© Copyright 2006 Integro Leadership Institute

Level 1. The Need to Be Respected: This is not rocket science; people need to be treated with *respect*. They need to be listened to and know that what they do is valued by their leaders. There are many ways leaders unintentionally treat employees with disrespect, and nothing *disengages* them faster.

Level 2. The Need to Learn and Grow: People have a natural desire to develop their talents and do things that utilize their strengths. They want to perform at their best. To do that, they need to continue to *learn and grow* in their roles.

Level 3. The Need to Be an Insider: No one likes to feel left out. Feeling judged or that you are being treated differently kills *engagement* and *passion*. Great leaders believe in people and make them aware of their significance.

Level 4. The Need for Meaning: People need to know that what they do is meaningful, that it makes a difference. They need to understand the purpose behind what they do and how it contributes to their organization's success.

Level 5. The Need to Be Part of a Winning Team: Being a part of and contributing to the success of a *winning team* generates *team spirit*. *High-performance teams* significantly outperform other similar teams because they are fueled by a shared *passion* for what they do. *Toyota – Solving problems on the line – at the level of the line.*

While defining these needs is straightforward, many leaders do not possess the necessary leadership skills to meet them. If they did, the level of *engagement* in the workforce would be much higher than it is. Leaders need a path to follow to develop the foundational beliefs and skills they need to succeed. This book provides that path in the form of a four-step process.

Four Steps to Success

Step 1 – Awareness: Without *awareness*, you are fumbling in the dark. When you are aware of why people are not *engaged* and what can be done to light a fire within them, you are then able to make the appropriate leadership choices. One of the most valuable ways I have found to increase my own and my clients' *self-awareness* is through valid, reliable *learning instruments*. A *learning instrument* is not a test—*you cannot pass or fail!* It is a questionnaire that allows you to give feedback to yourself. It holds up a mirror that shows you, without judgment, what you are currently doing and helps you understand what is working for you and what is not. More than increasing *self-awareness,* understanding the concepts behind these tools give you increased *awareness* of other people and why they do what they do.

For over twenty years, I have used a range of *learning instruments* from Minneapolis-based Inscape Publishing, Inc. with all of my clients. I use them because they work. Inscape has a strong commitment to quality and their ongoing research ensures they stay at the top of their field. With their permission, I have described in detail the concepts behind a number of their *learning instruments* throughout this book, because the increased *awareness* they provide speeds up the process of developing leadership skills and the resultant increase in employee commitment. If, after learning about these concepts, you are interested in getting more information about the *learning instruments*, go to the last page in the book for a list of resources.

Step 2 – Understanding: *Awareness* leads to *understanding*. To be effective in getting the best out of your team, you need to *understand* each of your team members and what he or she needs to be *passionate* about helping you achieve your dream. As each idea is explored, I have given examples that demonstrate how these concepts have an impact on people and their feelings about their work environment.

Step 3 – Methodology: There are many techniques presented in this book: how to recognize different *behavioral styles* in other people, how to *build trust* with people who are different from you, how to adapt your *listening approach*, and how to build a *high-performance team*, to name a few. You need the *awareness* and *understanding* to be able to apply the methodology.

Step 4 – Commitment: The *commitment* must come from you! Without your *commitment* to follow through and apply what you are learning, these skills cannot be developed, and the results from a *passionate, committed* team cannot be achieved.

A few words about the organization and intent of this book: It is structured into three sections and I will ask you a lot of questions. How you answer them determines your next course of action. I truly hope that you take the time to answer them.

Section I: *The Anatomy of a Leader* asks you to look at yourself as a leader. Chapter 1 challenges you to think about why you want to be a leader and how your *needs* and *values* affect your behavior as a leader. In Chapter 2, you will learn what leadership approach gets employees who are more *compliant* or *rebellious* to become *self-directed,* and keep them that way. And in Chapter 3, you will find the answer to why, even though you are trustworthy, some people don't trust you or question your motives.

Section II: *Getting Started on Engagement* focuses on the basic knowledge and skills leaders need to get people *engaged.* Chapter 4 outlines four *people skills* that are essential for building successful relationships based on a high level of *trust.* In Chapter 5, I will share with you a behavioral model I have found very helpful in understanding *what makes people tick.* Then in Chapter 6, we look at ten factors that take the mystery out of dealing with people who are different from you. Chapter 7 focuses on the *hidden motivator: values.* People are more *passion-*

ate about what they believe in and what they *value* than they will ever be about compensation and benefits.

Section III: *From Engagement to Passion* lays out the path to follow to develop the leadership skills needed to meet the needs that ignite *passion*. Chapters 8 through 12 cover each of the leadership skills that will help you meet the five levels of needs previously described and turn your team into a *high-performance team*.

Human beings are complex, and yet their needs for becoming *committed, passionate* team members are simple to understand. The leadership skills you need to ignite that fire within them are not that complex, but because they do not come naturally to most of us, they have to be learned. The reward for your willingness to do just that awaits you.

Enjoy the journey,
Keith E. Ayers

THE **ANATOMY** OF A **LEADER**

Leaders create the work environment their teams operate in every day. What kind of leadership do you need to provide to get the results you want from your team?

Leadership That Ignites Passion

I met David McNally, a striking-looking individual and one of the founders of Integro in Australia, at a sales conference in Melbourne in late 1976. Over a couple of drinks, we had a conversation that changed, and continues to shape, my life. David founded Integro about six months before we met to help clients achieve their business goals, but our talk at first centered on the usual salesman banter we've all had at these sorts of conferences. I could not stop asking him questions about his new business; the idea that the success an organization achieves is dependent on the degree to which their employees and customers trust them fascinated me. The more David explained Integro to me, and the excitement and passion with which he did it, the more interested and enthralled I became. I was so completely sold on the idea that at one point in our conversation—and it wasn't the beer talking—I just blurted out, "I'd love to do what you do!"

His response was calm and simple. "Why don't you?"

I was taken aback. At that point in my life, public speaking terrified me. My sales experience was limited. To see myself as capable of selling consulting and training services to organizations was a big stretch, something I did not feel ready for or confident enough to take on. David listened to me and let me speak, but as I came up with all the reasons why I couldn't do it, he nodded as though he had heard those reasons before—perhaps in his own head before he formed Integro—and considered them poor excuses.

Finally, David interrupted me. "You know, if you wait until you are ready, you'll be waiting the rest of your life. If this is something you really want to do, then you'll learn much faster by doing it. My motto is: Bite off more than you can chew, and chew like hell!"

He was right. Two months later, I joined Integro. That initial self-doubt remained with me early on, but I grew out of it. I'm still here today, in fact, now the President of Integro because David saw some talent in me I had yet to see in myself. He was a true leader. Leaders recognize the talent others have and create opportunities for them to develop that talent and become the leaders they are capable of being. David invested in me because he saw someone who could help him realize his vision for Integro. His passion did not stop at his vision for Integro; he was passionate about helping people grow. His leadership helped instill that passion in me. I was, and am, forever grateful for that random conversation at the sales conference because that day I was challenged to become a leader.

Why Do You Want to Be a Leader?

It is an important question to ask yourself. Obviously, you like the prestige and status of the position and the power it brings; the higher up you are in the organization, the more control you have over the direction you go and the decisions made. But the benefits of leadership—things like increased control and greater compensation—are not ends in themselves. There must be some other motive beyond what you *get* out of being a leader. I suspect you already possess this motive if you are reading this book, so you also understand, like David and I, that there are goals beyond your own that determine your success as a leader.

You have to *give* something of value to others to *get* the rewards of being a leader. It's called the **Give-Get Cycle**.

The Give-Get Cycle

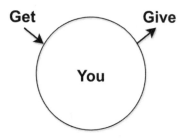

Whether you lead a team, business unit, department, or the whole organization, your leadership role was created for a reason. Your role or position has a *purpose*, and that is to deliver output your organization needs to achieve its strategic objectives. The more effective you are as a leader, the more you *give* of your leadership talents, the more your team will deliver to the organization, and the more you will *get* in both rewards and satisfaction. From now on, I will use the word "team" to describe the group of people you lead. Whether your team is three people or a thousand people, the same principles apply.

What Kinds of People Do You Need on Your Team to Be Successful as a Leader?

Pause for a moment and think about this question; it is a critical question all leaders must answer. You need to be very clear about the *kinds of people* you need to create a work environment which attracts and retains these people. There are many leaders who are unintentionally and unwittingly creating an environment that drives away the very people they need and, in the process, diminishing their results.

Every time I ask leaders this question about *kinds of people* I get the same answers. In addition to having team members with talent and skill, you also want motivated self-starters who are team players, results-oriented, engaged, talented, committed, responsible, innovative, willing to learn, and embrace change. How would you rate your team today against these criteria? How many team members are all these things all the time? Are they all engaged? Committed? Talented? How many are some of these things some of the time? How many match very few of these things? How many of them could be these things?

Remember, everyone on your team is potentially passionate about what he or she does. This goes beyond mere engagement. When people are passionate, their hearts are in concert with their minds as they are committed to their goals and inspired to work at their best every day. How passionate they are depends on you, the leader. What kind of work environment do you need to create to get your team to be passionate all the time? How do you attract and retain talented, committed people? How much of this is solely up to you? Let's have a look at an organization that has done these things.

Lighting a Fire Within

In early 2003, Unity Health Center was created out of a merger between two competing hospitals in Shawnee, Oklahoma. The primary goal of this merger was to convince Shawnee residents they did not need to travel to Oklahoma City to get quality healthcare. Like many healthcare facilities across the country, Unity

Health experienced a high level of turnover and had difficulty filling vacated positions. In 2002, there was an average of six to eight vacancies in each of six operating divisions that could not be filled. This led to the hospital being short-staffed by between forty and fifty people at a time, with the bulk of the short-staffing in nursing and support positions.

Said CEO Chuck Skillings at the time, "We needed to cease being competitors and become collaborators, united in our mission and vision. The name 'Unity Health Center' is a reflection of the spirit of unification that happens daily in a hospital, when groups of individuals such as doctors and nurses combine talents, abilities, and training to help others. We are committed to bringing technology and compassion together to fulfill our mission statement: Positively impacting human life through exceptional healthcare."

To realize this new mission, hospital leaders at all levels had to create a work environment where all employees were empowered to make a positive difference in the lives and health of those they served.

Dawn Klinglesmith was the Director of Diagnostic Imaging at Unity Health at the time. She, like many healthcare managers, dealt with life and death situations every day. "My typical day was focused on directing and managing people. They would come to me with their problems and, of course, I would try and fix them. If they came to me for a decision, I would make it. I hadn't really thought about the difference between leadership and management."

This is a critical distinction. Dawn was initially skeptical about embracing the Integro leadership development process. She feared she would lose time that she just did not have by attending sessions instead of concentrating on her more important duties. This leadership process was a long-term commitment that included meeting with her staff in both group and one-on-one meetings and required Dawn to apply the principles in real-time at the hospital. Fortunately, she did it with an open mind and, over the next few months, she started to see differences in the way staff interacted with patients and in her own leadership approach.

Now when team members approached her with a problem, she did not simply tell them the solution and expect them to act it out. Instead, she asked them what they thought was the best solution, then helped them determine their course of action. A new and empowered team was born—one that made decisions, led initiatives, and felt ownership and passion for their work.

Dawn summed up her experience after the Integro leadership process: "Learning to lead by building trust and personal responsibility has truly changed the way I communicate with my team. It has left a positive imprint on my personal life as well as with the staff I interact with on a daily basis. I learned so many priceless lessons to take back and instill in my day-to-day interactions with my team. *I no longer light a fire under my staff, I light a fire in them*, and it truly has made all the difference in the world. Rather than focus on managing people, I now operate by my personal mission statement: To create an environment where people can be their best."

The results for Unity Health Center have been dramatic. With leadership focused on working with employees to fulfill their mission, staff vacancies decreased from a consistent forty to fifty positions three years ago to a negligible level. The impact on the organization's ability to fulfill its purpose was very positive. And all of it was accomplished with the same core group of people.

So, what changed? *Leadership behavior.* The leadership team changed their focus from managing and controlling people to one of working in partnership with employees. They were presented with the challenge: "How can we better positively impact human life through exceptional healthcare?" The employees rose to the challenge and took responsibility for making the new mission statement real, and the results have been truly outstanding.

The Whole Person Concept

To create an environment like Dawn did at Unity Health, you need to assess your own leadership style and how it impacts the environment your team experiences. Are you even aware of how your team perceives your behavior? Everything you do at work impacts the environment you create. The best leaders can take a step back and look at themselves objectively. You must do that, too.

Have you ever noticed that wherever you go, there you are…all of you? This is not some existential question designed to confuse you. Take it literally. You know you cannot leave part of yourself at home when you go to work. You are a *whole person*. The **Whole Person Concept** is a simple way of understanding what you take with you everywhere you go and how others see you. I also refer to the **Whole Person Concept** as the *iceberg model*, because, as you can see in the graphic, people have a lot in common with an iceberg.

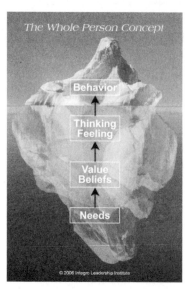

Scientists say only about one-seventh of the entire mass, just the tip of the iceberg, is obvious and visible above the waterline; the rest is beneath the surface. People are like that too.

There are four aspects to the **Whole Person Concept**: *behavior, thinking and feeling, values and beliefs,* and *needs.*

BEHAVIOR

It makes sense to start with the tip of the iceberg because that is what everybody else can see. When you meet people for the first time, all you can see is their *behavior*; you really don't know anything else about them. You only have their *behavior* by which to attempt to understand them and figure out how you want to relate to them. There is so much more to people than their *behavior*, so many aspects below the waterline that you can't see. I am sure you can think of people who are a mystery to you. You look at them and silently ask yourself, *"Why do they do that? That just doesn't make any sense to me."*

They don't make sense to you because what's going on inside them is very different to what goes on inside you. So, if you are going to be a leader who creates an environment that ignites passion, you need to understand your *behavior*, and what is going on inside you that drives it. This will also help you understand how your *behavior* can be interpreted or misinterpreted by people who are different from you, who look at your *behavior* and say, *"Why does she do that? Why does he behave the way he does?"*

The law of vibration
The law of Attraction

THINKING AND FEELING

Everything you do is done because you either *think* you should do it, or because you *feel* like you want to do it. The *thinking and feeling* aspect lies just below the waterline of the **Whole Person Concept**. In many ways, *thinking* and *feeling* are inseparable. When you *think* about something, you have *feelings* associated with that thought. When you *think* about something you love to do, hopefully your work, you *feel* energized and enthusiastic. But when you *think* about something you hate to do, hopefully not your work, you experience *feelings* of dread and desire to avoid doing it.

You also have *thoughts* about your *feelings*. When you are *feeling* angry with people, you are likely to be *thinking* about all the reasons why you should be angry with them, why they should not have done what they did. Or, you could be questioning your *feelings*: *Why am I getting so angry over something so insignificant?*

Attracting more like thoughts

Even though they are so closely linked, *thinking* and *feeling* can come into conflict. Have you ever woken up and not *felt* like getting out of bed? That question is rhetorical; of course you have. What do you do? Do you hit the snooze button and go back to sleep because that is what you *feel* like doing, or do you drag yourself out of bed and get ready for work because you *think* you should? Hopefully, your *feelings* about facing the day change by the time you get to work. If not, then what does your employer or customer get from you? Someone who is going through the motions with no enthusiasm, no commitment, and certainly no passion!

At the University of Queensland in Brisbane, Australia, I was a sprinter and 220-yard hurdler on the track team. At training one night the week before the National Inter-Varsity Championships, I had absolutely zero motivation to train. I told my coach how I was *feeling*, and, being the wise coach that he was, he suggested I jog a few laps to warm up and then see how I *felt*. He was right! After a few laps and some short sprints, I really *felt* like training and had a great workout. The same idea probably holds true for you when you don't *feel* like going to the gym to work out. You *think* you should and, once you get there, most of the time you are glad you did it. Start doing what you know you should be doing and let your *feelings* catch up. But always be aware of how your *thinking* and *feeling* are affecting your behavior.

what is your vibration - frequency

VALUES AND BELIEFS

We are more complex than merely our thinking, feeling, and behavior. Deeper motives stir within us: our *values* and *beliefs*. Like thinking and feeling, they are interconnected. A *value* is something you believe in, and it serves as a compass to how you think and feel. If you *value* honesty, then you no doubt have established

Preset Thermostat   *Cybernetics*

beliefs about what honesty is, what it means to you, and what you believe to be right or wrong. When someone does something wrong according to your standards of honesty, it impacts how you feel and think about that person, and maybe how you behave towards him or her as well. *A belief is a thought you have practiced over and over until in becomes programmed.*

The difference between a *belief* and a thought is that *beliefs* are thoughts that become fact to you. When you first hear something, you mull it over a bit then decide upon its validity as a truthful statement. You say, *"I agree with that. It's a fact."* Once you've made that decision, it is no longer just a thought, it is a *belief. Beliefs* are much deeper down in the iceberg than thoughts. They are more personal and exist closer to the core of your being. You make decisions based on your *beliefs* and *values* all the time without questioning them.

But *beliefs* are not always right. Perhaps the most glaring example of a false *belief* occurred in Europe just before the Renaissance when, until the publication of ***De revolutionibus orbium coelestium*** in 1530 by Nicolas Copernicus, people *believed* the earth was a fixed, immovable mass located at the center of the universe with the sun and stars revolving around it. Copernicus refuted this *belief*, citing astronomical and mathematical evidence that the earth revolved around the sun, but he did not publish his work at the time because it went against the philosophical and religious teaching of the time that mankind was the center of the universe.

After his death, two other Italian scientists, Galileo and Giordano Bruno, published work based on Copernican theory only to find that the Church was not ready to *believe* it. Bruno was burned at the stake in 1600 and Galileo imprisoned for life, albeit comfortably, in 1633. The world leaders at that time operated on *beliefs* that were false, but they were so convinced they were right that they rejected any and all alternate views. Of course, we now have scientific evidence that the sun is the center of our solar system, but the fact that people stubbornly held on to their *beliefs* for so long, even though they were false, shows how our *beliefs* can potentially stand in the way of progress. *Limiting beliefs*

What are your *beliefs* about what it takes to be a leader and achieve outstanding results? If some of your *beliefs* have actually prevented you from getting the best possible performance out of your team or organization, are you willing to question what you *believe* to be true? I'm not asking you to throw out your *beliefs*. What I am suggesting is that there is real value in being open-minded enough to question your *beliefs*. If you are right, you will be even more certain of it by being open to the idea of maybe being wrong. Differences in *values* and *beliefs* are the cause of so much unnecessary conflict in the world. It is very important to understand that if someone else's beliefs vary from your own, it does not mean that person is wrong and you are right. It *may* be that you are right. It may be that you

Are they in alignment / do they support the kind of leader you desire to be.

34

are *both* right. But is it more important to be right, or to be effective as a leader?

To be an effective leader you must understand the **Whole Person Concept** if you hope to ignite people's passion. People are more passionate about something they believe in, so aligning their *personal values* with your *organizational values* is an important aspect of your leadership role.

NEEDS

At the bottom of the iceberg, at our core, are our *needs*. *Needs* are the most instinctive part of us. These are necessities like eating, drinking, and breathing that spring from something primal in us all. Eating is a good example of how our *needs* connect with our behavior, thinking and feeling, and values and beliefs. When we are hungry, we eat. Eating is the behavior that satisfies our *need*. Sometimes these *needs* are filtered by your beliefs and values before you act to satisfy them. When you're hungry, you don't necessarily grab the first edible thing in sight because you feel like it. You may think it is not good for you, so you temper your *need*, but the *need* to eat is there, nonetheless, and must be satisfied.

Some *needs* are more instinctive and go straight through from *needs* to feelings to behavior, skipping values and beliefs altogether. None of us is born with values and beliefs because the cognitive thinking part of the brain is not yet functional at that age; we have no language, only primal *needs*, feelings, and behavior. As babies, when our *needs* were satisfied, we felt happy, content with sleeping, playing, laughing, crawling around, and just being inquisitive. When our *needs* were not met, however, we were not satisfied and acted accordingly—in other words, we cried.

Unfortunately, some adults still operate in such a basic and primal way. They do not think about their actions, they merely react to their *needs* and feelings without having learned to manage their emotions. Yelling and screaming at people is inappropriate behavior in the workplace or, for that matter, anywhere. It accomplishes nothing positive in the long term, especially if the goal is to get employees to be more passionate, yet I hear stories all the time about managers who yell and scream to get employees to do what they say. Why? To regain control when they feel they are losing control. They are control freaks! Those who work with them will do just about anything to make sure they don't yell and scream again. So it works—in the short term. People who scream at other people are a liability to the organization, no matter what they are producing.

Two Sources of Motivation

We will revisit this **Whole Person Concept** frequently throughout the book because it is a critical foundational model for being an effective leader. But first, you need to understand your own behavior and its two sources of motivation.

Needs Motivation is doing what makes you happy, makes you money, gets you recognition, gets you affection, earns you respect, or achieves results. It is the *get* part of the **Give-Get Cycle**. Unsatisfied needs create compulsive behavior, driving you to meet that need at all costs. The only way you can satisfy your own needs is through your own behavior, even if that need is going to be satisfied by someone else. For example, we all need affection from time to time. The way to *get* this need satisfied is not by sitting around, waiting for someone to *give* it to you. You meet the need by *giving* to *get*, by doing something that will *get* someone else to *give* you affection. This applies to any need you have. You have to *give* something to *get* the need satisfied. *Giving to Get example: a hug*

Values Motivation is doing what you believe you should do, what you believe is right, and what you believe is appropriate. It may not suit your short-term needs at the time—as we saw with Dawn's reaction to having to focus on leadership and staff development that took her away from performing other duties at the hospital—but it will serve you in the long haul. It is not uncommon to have some internal conflict between needs and values.

Because your behavior creates the environment your team works in, you need to understand what your *needs* and *values* are, how they influence your *thinking* and *feeling*, and ultimately your *behavior*. If you want your team to be passionate about their work and give their best every day, then you must start with your own *behavior*. The next two chapters focus on the impact your behavior as a leader has on your team members' willingness to be accountable and the level of trust in your team. Then we will go below the waterline to understand the needs and values of your team members to find out what ignites their passion.

Why Won't They Be Responsible?

When I first moved from Australia to Pennsylvania in 2001 to expand Integro into the United States, my wife, Kelley, and I were not certain how long our stay would be. Integro was very successful in Australia, and making the leap to America was the next logical step, but we were cautious about our commitment. Because of this, we rented a house instead of buying one. The rental contract included a monthly cleaning service.

After a long day at the office a few months after moving in, I pulled into our driveway only to find that the garage door that worked every day until then would not open. It tried to open when I pushed the remote opener, revving like it wanted to rise, but it didn't. I got out of my car, went into the house through the front door, and discovered the problem: the garage door was manually locked from the inside. This happened the same day the cleaners were there, so I called the cleaning contractor to suggest she advise her staff not to lock the garage door again from the inside. To my surprise, she immediately denied it could have been anyone on her staff that locked the door because, she said, "My cleaning staff knows how to operate automatic doors!" She didn't even ask them about it and was simply unwilling to accept responsibility, much less provide effective customer service.

Has anything like that ever happened to you? If it has, I'm sure you were just as frustrated and furious as I was, especially after I got the repair bill for the garage door motor. But the cleaners did a good job, and dependable contractors are hard to find, so I overlooked the incident. A few months later, I again pulled into my driveway and tried to open the garage door, but the door wouldn't open. It was locked from inside. Yes, the cleaners were there again that day, but this time the door buckled badly under the strain and needed to be replaced. I called the cleaning contractor, and again she refused to accept any responsibility, leaving me with a larger repair bill and a reminder not to count on someone who does not accept *personal responsibility*. We replaced the cleaners with someone more responsible, who does a great job and does not lock the door from the inside.

Accountability is rarely an issue when your team performs well. It is when something goes awry that *accountability* becomes a thorny issue, and that is what gives the word its negative connotation. It happened with my former cleaning people, and they put forth the idea in my mind that the failure to accept *accountability* is how we define excuses. In your role as a leader, how do you get every one of your team members to be *accountable* when so many people these days seem to want to avoid responsibility, especially for results? Aren't they always looking for someone or something to blame? If simply holding people *accountable* worked, then I would not have had to pay for the damage to my garage door.

Respond
Just
Blame
Shame

Accountability is a choice. **People will not be accountable until they choose to be accountable.** If you do not understand that, you will not succeed at getting everyone on your team to be *accountable*. I find it helpful to distinguish between *responsibility* and *accountability* this way: *responsibility* is an attitude, belief, or state of mind that you choose; *accountability* is the outcome or what you do once you have taken *responsibility*.

We will address two aspects of *personal responsibility* in this chapter.

First, there is your *personal responsibility* as a leader for the environment you create and the quality and appropriateness of the leadership you provide. Second, we will explore what it takes to get other people to willingly take responsibility, especially those people who want to avoid it.

The Personal Responsibility Model

The **Personal Responsibility Model** looks at whether people operate as *other-directed* or *self-directed. Other-directed* people believe they have no control over their own lives and instead are controlled by people in authority. For an *other-directed* person, the locus of control is external to himself. On the other hand, the *self-directed* person sees the locus of control as internal: *I have control of my life. Self-directed* people see themselves as autonomous, which comes from the ancient Greek words "auto," meaning "self," and "nomos," meaning "law." So, they are a law unto themselves—literally. The basic underlying belief of the *other-directed* person is *I have to*, meaning there is no belief about choice other than what the authority says. For the *self-directed* person, the belief is *I choose to*. They believe they always have choice.

Live your life by Creation or Default —
Leader or Follower —

Personal Responsibility

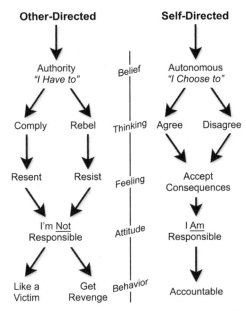

Look at the graphic and you'll see we begin with the *beliefs* people have based on their decisions about whether or not they have control over their lives. As we saw with the **Whole Person Concept** in the previous chapter, *beliefs* have a strong impact on your *thinking* and *feeling*, which determines your *attitude*. Your *attitude* results in a corresponding *behavior*. We'll start with the *other-directed* side, and then return to look at the right hand side of the model, the *self-directed* side.

Chances are, you will recognize some of this behavior in your organization.

OTHER-DIRECTED BEHAVIOR

When you give *other-directed* people a new task to do that is not already in their job description, they view it with an *"I have to"* frame of mind. They make one of two choices: *comply,* and do as they are told; or *rebel,* and say, *"This isn't my job. Why should I have to do this?"* The vibration at which they do it is what poisons.

When employees *comply* and do something they do not want to do or feel they have no choice about doing, the natural feeling is to *resent* the authority for making them do it. Even though they will eventually do the task, they do it grudgingly, and only well enough to not get into trouble. The *compliant* person does not attempt to do the job as well as they can—it's just a job they <u>have to</u> do.

When employees' thinking is to *rebel,* they resist doing the work. Typically, when people resist doing something, they don't usually come out and say, *"I am not going to do it."* They just never get it done. *Rebellious* employees get some work done because they need to keep their jobs, but they can at the same time be undermining what the *self-directed* employees are achieving.

Whether *other-directed* people *comply* or *rebel*, their attitude is: *I am not responsible.* They either behave like *victims,* feeling sorry for themselves and whining to their friends and co-workers about you as a boss, or they plot *revenge.* Sometimes it's both. In either instance, their intention is to undermine what you want to accomplish.

The ways in which *other-directed* employees get *revenge* range from slowing down on their work output, to sabotaging projects, to calling in sick when they are not, even stealing things. The kind of *revenge* employees seek will depend on whether they want to *get even* with the organization as a whole, or just their immediate manager. The most common form of *revenge,* however, is holding back on giving their best performance.

On a scale of one to ten, how much of their best do you get from your staff? Think about how many of your team members do just enough to keep their jobs in your organization? How much can they get away with? When I have polled managers about this, the average score is between 4 and 5. In smaller organizations, the average of 5 or 6 implies that employees give more of their best. In larger organizations, the number is as low as 2 or 3. It is so easy for people to hold back from giving their best and stay out of trouble. All they have to do is switch off. It's called *disengagement!*

Why do people switch off? Look at the model. When people believe they have no control, that they are being controlled by the authorities in their lives, they feel that they have no choice other than to *comply* or *rebel.* We learn as children to be *other-directed* because of all the people in our lives we are expected to *comply* with: parents, teachers, preachers, and no doubt many other adults, even the local shopkeeper. Everyone is an authority when you are a child; children require structure and guidance, so some of that authoritarian influence from elders is essential. Authoritarian behavior creates *other-directed* reactions.

My parents were Salvation Army missionaries. I spent the first six years of my life in the West Indies, Central America, and Dutch Guiana (now Suriname). When I was five, we lived in Paramaribo in Suriname, and like most places in the tropics, there were seasonal, monsoon rains. On both sides of the road ran monsoon drains that were about five feet deep, ten feet wide at the top, and tapered down to about three feet at the bottom. Our house was on an acre of land so, when my older brother, Kevin, and I got bikes for Christmas, we had a lot of space for riding. My father was strict, making it very clear that we were not to go outside the gate of our yard on our bikes. At that age, when someone told me not to do something, it felt like a challenge. I just had to do it. My tendency was to *rebel!*

One day when my father was out, I rode my bike outside the gate and across the bridge where our car would drive over the monsoon drain and down along the side of the road to another little narrow pedestrian bridge which came to our front gate. Because I was in a hurry, I lost my balance going over the narrow bridge, rode straight over the side, and fell down into the monsoon drain, which, at that point in time, was about a foot deep with green slime. The last thing I remember was standing in the bathtub as my mother mopped me down to get rid of all the slime. "Just wait until your father gets home," she said. It seemed each time I rebelled, I got caught. That didn't stop me, however. The stricter my father was, particularly because he gave me no real reason as to why he was so strict, the more I rebelled. Had my father said to my brother and me, "If you leave the yard, you could get killed," then maybe I would have listened. But then, maybe not. I don't think I would have believed him.

SELF-DIRECTED BEHAVIOR Take 100% responsibility

The central difference between *other-directed* and *self-directed* team members is that *self-directed* people believe at all times that they *have a choice*. When you ask *self-directed* employees to do a new task, their thinking is to either *agree* or *disagree* with doing it. If they *agree* to do the task, then they will do it to the best of their ability, *because it is their choice*. If they *disagree*, they will explain to their manager the reasons why they *disagree*. Either way, the feeling that *self-directed* people have is one of *acceptance* of whatever the outcomes are of their decisions. They *accept the consequences* of their decisions and actions because they feel ownership of them. If *self-directed* team members agree to do a job and do not do it to expected standards, then they will *accept the consequences* for not having given their best. If they *disagree* with the task, and there are negative consequences for doing so, they will *accept these consequences*, too. If they lose their jobs, they take responsibility for it; it's not the responsibility of the boss or the company. They understand that if you make a decision that results in you losing your job, you are responsible for the outcome. That's what *self-directed* people do. Prior to making decisions they consider the consequences of the decision, then act based on their understanding of those consequences.

Sometimes, our decisions result in negative consequences that we could not have foreseen. This is a fact of life. The *self-directed* person remains responsible for the outcome regardless.

In Chapter 1, I asked you what *kinds of people* you need on your team to fulfill your purpose. Think about the answers you came up with and I'm sure you will see that they fit into the *self-directed* side of this model. Every leader in every organization that I have spoken with wants *self-directed* people. But even though

41

that is what they want, many managers behave in a way that prevents them from having what they want. If you behave in an authoritarian way, demanding or expecting *compliance*, you will end up with *other-directed* people. *Self-directed* people need to have a choice. Give them no choice and they will choose to work somewhere else. *Entrepreneur may say – I don't have to give them a choice really. They aren't the ones who will loose Big if their way doesn't work.*

Authoritarian behavior does not work. If you seek to control *self-directed* people, to make them *comply*, they will either give up and become *other-directed*, or they will leave. When they give up, they will either *comply* with your demands and lose their spirit, or they will *rebel*. *In order to tolerate, you have to disconnect.*

There are examples of this in all areas of society. Parents want their children to be responsible and accountable but use authoritarian behavior in their attempt to accomplish it. They do not want to give their children too much freedom, but they also expect them to be responsible, so when their children *rebel*, parents wonder what's gone wrong. Usually they wonder what is wrong with their children rather than look at their own approach to parenting. They fail to ask themselves, *"Am I causing this? Is my authoritarian behavior resulting in rebellion, resentment, or victim-like behavior?"*

Anytime you use authoritarian behavior in an attempt to force people to *comply* with what you want, you are risking the danger of creating *resentment* and *revengeful* behavior. This applies to everyone in a leadership role—in business, at home, at school, and at church.

Learned Helplessness

Some people behave in an *other-directed* way because they have never learned to be *self-directed*. Children who grow up authoritarian homes, attend authoritarian schools, and belong to authoritarian churches never have any real choices. Chances are that when they leave home, they are going to look for an authoritarian organization where they do not have to make decisions and will be told what to do. They never learn to think for themselves. In his book **Learned Optimism**, Dr. Martin Seligman from the University of Pennsylvania talks about people who *learn helplessness*. The good news about *learned helplessness* is that it can be unlearned, hence the title **Learned Optimism**[6]. Even people who never became *self-directed* in their youth can learn to become *self-directed* as adults.

E+R=O

How Early Can Children Learn to Be Self-Directed?

I have a friend in Hawaii, Sarah, who has a son, Trey. From early on in her son's life, Sarah let him know that in any situation he had choices, and that there are outcomes for each choice he makes. For example, if it was bedtime and he didn't want to go, Sarah explained his choices: 1) Go to bed now, or 2) Stay up late. Sarah would ask him to think about the consequences of what might happen if he went to bed late when he had kindergarten the next morning. He knew from experience how unpleasant it would be if he went to kindergarten really tired. As a result, Sarah's son was able to participate in a *self-directed* decision making process at just four years of age. However, it doesn't always work.

One day, Sarah and her son were at the playground and he was at the top of a climbing apparatus. Sarah had told him a couple of times that it was time to come down, but, just like most four year olds, he kept on playing. And just like most parents in a situation like this, Sarah's patience wore a bit thin and she declared, "You just do what I say." Her son stopped, looked down at her, and defiantly said, "What are my choices?" Sarah answered, "You have no choice—just get down here!" Trey responded by saying, "You said we always have choices." Even at four years of age, Sarah's son learned he had choices, but he still had more to learn about thinking through the consequences.

Sarah's experience with her son is exactly what you need to do with team members who are not *self-directed*. When people come to you with a problem, do what Dawn did at Unity Health: ask them to define the problem, then, rather than make the decision for them, ask them what they think the best solution is. You may recognize this as the Socratic Method. If a team member answers that he doesn't know, ask him to think through the possible solutions and what the likely outcome of each would be. Encourage him to use his problem-solving abilities and ask him to come back to you with the options. This is your first step toward creating more *self-directed* employees. *Other-directed* people tend not to think through the options and what the consequences for each might be. By helping them do that, you can build their confidence in themselves and have them wanting to take on more responsibility in the organization.

Solving problems and making decisions for others who are capable of doing it themselves robs them of the chance to become *self-directed*. You rob them of the satisfaction of using their own talents and experience to make decisions. If they don't know how to do something, you have the opportunity to help them learn.

At the beginning of this chapter, I indicated that we would be looking at two aspects of *personal responsibility*: yours and your team members.

So far, we've focused more on team members. To what extent are you operating in a *self-directed* way, accepting responsibility for the decisions you make and for the way you behave? To what extent are you accepting responsibility for the environment in which your team members currently work? As a leader, are you using authoritarian behavior to demand or expect *compliance*? Do you give people any *choice* about what they do and how they do it? When you use authoritarian behavior, you are operating on the *other-directed* side, too, even though you may think you are being *self-directed*.

self directed
Often times - a other directed person who feels undervalued/disrespected - disengages ⇒ says "well go ahead and do it his way and when it doesn't work - then he'll get what he deserves.

43

Passionate employees who come to work and give their best every day are not *other-directed*. Presuming you agree that you need *self-directed* people on your team, what do you do with those team members who avoid responsibility and accountability? Remember, most people do not join an organization with the intention of being *other-directed*. They want to make a difference, which is what interested them in the position in the first place. If they are now behaving in an *other-directed* way, the work environment or culture no doubt had a part to play in them becoming that way.

The first step to increasing responsibility and accountability is to ensure that you have a culture or environment where your team members not only <u>can</u> be, but also <u>want</u> to be *self-directed*.

The Responsibility-Based Culture

	Authority-Driven	Responsibility-Based
Level of Trust	*Trust is Low*	*Trust is Essential*
Leadership Approach	*Control Based... Ensure Compliance*	*Believe in People- Partner with them*
Who is Responsible?	*Nobody wants to be... They play the Blame Game*	*Everyone wants to own their job*
Employee Behavior... (Kinds of People)	*Other-Directed Not-Engaged*	*Self-Directed Engaged*

The Responsibility-Based Culture Model

The **Responsibility-Based Culture Model** contrasts an *authority-driven* environment with a *responsibility-based* environment by looking at four specific elements: *level of trust, leadership approach, who is responsible,* and *kinds of people.*

LEVEL OF TRUST

In an *authority-driven* environment where leaders make all the decisions and expect people to carry them out, *trust is low*. This environment conveys the message that team members cannot be trusted to make decisions or think for themselves. When managers micromanage, the essential message they send to team members is: "*I don't trust you to work on your own.*" Security cameras focused on employees, punch cards for employees to clock in and out, and monitoring employee email are other examples of ways organizations let employees know: "*We don't trust you.*"

The lack of trust goes both ways in an *authority-driven* environment. Employees don't trust managers who exercise complete control over them. How much can you trust someone who at any time can make a decision that adversely affects you, especially when past experience says it is likely to happen? How much do you trust someone who does not trust you?

In a *responsibility-based* environment, however, *trust must be high*. It is essential! Leaders will not allow people to take ownership of their jobs unless they trust them, and employees are not going to take responsibility unless they trust their leaders. The reason so many employees avoid responsibility is that they fear negative consequences from being responsible. If their experience is that mistakes are not tolerated, there is even more reason to avoid responsibility. In that environment, the one who is responsible is the one who gets the blame. The starting point for creating a work environment where people will be passionate about what they do is to *build trust!*

LEADERSHIP APPROACH

An *authority-driven* environment is *control-based*; it is designed to ensure *compliance.* In some organizations, *compliance* is achieved through strict adherence to policies, procedures, and rules; managers see their role as making sure that everyone follows the letter of the law. That way you know that everyone is doing everything right.

What's wrong with that?

Peter, the COO of a financial services organization in Sydney, Australia, had a primary business objective of obtaining market leadership through excellence in products and customer service. He expected very high standards from his operations and customer service staff. In the process, he created a policies and procedures manual which ensured there was absolutely no uncertainty about how to perform any task or process. Every "i" was dotted, every "t" crossed. His managers were held accountable for ensuring that all employees adhered to the policies and procedures. As a result, the employees primarily focused on sticking to the rules. Failure to do so resulted in a swift reprimand.

Soon, Peter was puzzled by the increasing level of customer complaints and subsequent loss of customers to competitors who were more innovative and responsive. In theory, his objective of providing excellent products and services was very appropriate. In practice, however, the strategic objective could not be achieved in the culture he cultivated. His focus on such strict adherence to a set of policies and procedures resulted in customers frequently being told their requests could not be met because of company policy. It never occurred to Peter that his frontline employees, the ones who had the most contact with the customers, knew more about what the customers wanted than anyone in the organization. They knew more about how to deliver customer satisfaction than he did. Peter never consulted them on the new policy before enacting it.

To have policies and procedures is not authoritarian; it is how they are administered and applied that is the issue. In an *authority-driven* environment, policies and procedures become the authority. Once they are established, the focus is on *compliance* without question, even when it does not make sense or will not achieve the best outcome. Blind *compliance* can be very detrimental to a workplace.

What if the policies and procedures do make sense and produce excellent results? What if it is just the law or a government regulation? Wouldn't it be logical to ensure that all employees understand so that they can choose to do the right thing? You don't need to coerce *self-directed* people into doing the right thing. In a *responsibility-based* environment, leaders ensure that employees understand what the choices are and potential consequences for each. Leaders *believe in* and *trust* people to do the right thing, and they educate people to ensure they can make the right choices for everyone involved. These leaders create a *partnership* with employees to make the best possible organization. Leaders in a *responsibility-based* organization also encourage employees to question or challenge any policy or procedure that doesn't make sense, doesn't work, or seems outdated or outmoded. This does not mean that employees have a right to change it, just that they can constructively question it. Then, if it does not make sense or is outdated, it should be changed by those who have the authority to do so.

Several years ago, while delivering a leadership presentation to the senior executive team of an organization that makes ear implants for deaf people, one of the executives said to me, "But you don't understand! The people in our clean rooms have to comply. They have to make each ear implant perfectly. We can't just let them do what they want!"

I replied, "Do you want the people making your implants to feel like they have to be perfect or they'll get into trouble? Or, do you want them to choose to make each one perfectly because they understand how meaningful their work is to the person who is hard of hearing who will receive it, and have great pride in what they do?"

Who is going to produce the best product: the fear driven *other-directed* employee or the *self-directed* one who is inspired to do his or her best? You know the answer. **Controlling people does not create accountability!** Other than in very specific circumstances, such as an emergency, *control-based* leadership achieves the opposite of accountability. Still, so many leaders believe control is working for them. My observation is that they think it is working for them because they are fortunate to have enough *self-directed* and accountable people around them that they achieve good results in spite of their controlling style. What these leaders fail to see is that the *rebellious* and *compliant* people on their team are taking away from what the *self-directed* people achieve—and preventing the team from achieving its real potential. So they continue to operate under the illusion that control works for them. The more controlling you are as a manager, the more *rebellious* and *compliant* people you will have and the more likely the *self-directed* people will want to leave. Stephen M. R. Covey

WHO IS RESPONSIBLE?

In an *authority-driven* environment no one wants to be *responsible* and everyone is pointing fingers at each other as the reason that goals were not met. Management blames employees for their lack of initiative. Employees blame management because they did not set the goals or have any input into how to achieve the result. As far as they are concerned, if they did not have a say in the setting of the goals or how to achieve them, it's not their fault if they are not achieved.

In a *responsibility-based* environment, all team members take *responsibility* for their decisions, actions, and results because they know the team's direction, and they have some stake in guiding them there. The *self-directed* employees working in the clean rooms making ear implants understand the purpose of what they do beyond the procedures they need to follow to produce a perfect result. Yes, they are aware of the policies and follow them, but they do it because they choose to and have no reason to resent them. They know by doing so, all organizational and personal goals are met. Best of all, they are helping deaf people to hear, which is the business they chose to enter in the first place.

KINDS OF PEOPLE

The *kinds of people* you have is a direct result of your leadership approach. People who are *compliant*, who are simply going through the motions, and people who are *rebellious*, who feel resentful, frustrated, or angry, are more focused on meeting their own needs than the organization's needs. A leadership approach based on *believing in people*, *trusting* them to do the right thing, and expecting them to be *responsible* and *accountable* will result in *self-directed* behavior. Your employees will not need to be supervised to perform at their best every day, which is a win-win situation for everyone involved. But it takes time. Just as it is ineffective to use a *control-based* approach with people who are *self-directed*, it is ineffective to empower an *other-directed* person. You cannot empower someone who does not want to be empowered any more than you can make someone be responsible who does not want responsibility. Until *mutual trust* is established, a *partnership-based* approach will not work. It's the **Give-Get Cycle**. You have to *give* trust before you can *get* it.

Once you've established trust and that trust is mutual, team members who were previously *other-directed* will take on much more responsibility than most managers would dream of. Why? Because they choose to. *Trust* must be the starting point.

Your Circle of Influence

You may think, *"This makes a lot of sense, but I work in a very control-based organization. How can I create a Responsibility-Based Culture?"* The reality is that most organizations in the world are *control-based*. This, I believe, is the primary reason that less than 30 percent of employees in the United States are *engaged*, and most other countries have even lower levels of engagement.

You may not be in the position to influence the creation of a *Responsibility-Based Culture* across your entire organization, but you can focus on your *circle of influence*. Start in places where you have some influence and with those whom you can influence. Are you being *self-directed?* Are you going to accept responsibility for the environment you create and for recreating it to achieve the best results your team is capable of? Or, are you going to be *other-directed*, make excuses, and blame the organization's culture for your inability to achieve what you are capable of?

What can you do?

The first step: **Stop playing authoritarian roles!** Because you cannot simply wave a magic wand and change people from *other-directed* to *self-directed*, phase out your authoritarian approach by slowly indoctrinating choice into your team's work. This will begin the trust process. You can start taking responsibility for the impact you may be having on the relationships in your team. If your team has *other-directed* people, are you willing to accept that you have contributed to the environment that supports the behaviors that you are now seeing from your team? I'm not suggesting that you alone are responsible. Some of your team may have been *other-directed* when you took your position. But have you allowed them to continue to be that way, or reinforced their behavior by attempting to control them? Are you willing to accept responsibility for changing the environment?

About six months into the process of creating a *Responsibility-Based Culture* at the AAA Club of South Jersey, the President of the Club, Carol Scott, was headed home from work, wondering about the challenges she was experiencing with some people in the organization. The lack of commitment from some people was very frustrating for her. Then it occurred to Carol that perhaps her behavior towards her team had contributed to the situation. The realization that changing her relationship with these team members required a change in her behavior toward them was a significant turning point for Carol. As a result, her relationships with her managers began to improve. In Carol's own words: "Not only are we building better relationships with our employees, our employees are building better relationships with our customers, and that is showing up in significant gains in our customer satisfaction scores."

$E + R = O$

Being *self-directed* means accepting the consequences of everything you do. If you don't like the results you are getting, look at what you are doing!

I'm sure you've heard this definition of insanity: *doing the same thing you have always done and expecting a different result!* Don't be insane in your relationships with people or your approach to managing them and getting results. Focus on what you need to do with your team to get them to a point where they are really passionate about coming to work and going to extreme lengths every day to do the best job they know how to do.

Remember, getting people who are currently *other-directed* to behave in a *self-directed* way will not happen overnight. It takes time and effort, and you have to *give* to *get*. But the more you *give*, and the more you trust your team to be responsible, the more you will *get* in return.

CHAPTER 3

Being Trustworthy Is Not Enough

Larry is the President of NuParts, Inc., a small manufacturing company that makes components. The business had good relationships with its customers for the twenty-five years they had been in business. However, increasing competition from overseas suppliers required the company to reduce their prices over the past two years. Larry was brought in by the owners to reduce costs so that pricing could be more competitive and profitability maintained.

Larry and his management team did an excellent job. They retained all of their key customers and their rigorous cost-cutting program maintained previous levels of profitability. The owners placed a lot of *trust* in Larry and he did a great job. They certainly saw him as *trustworthy!*

Beneath the surface, the picture at NuParts was not so rosy. One of the decisions made by Larry and the senior team to reduce costs was to lay off 10 percent of the workforce. They felt existing production levels could be maintained by the reduced workforce if they worked harder and smarter. Quality suffered a little since the layoffs, with defective parts increasing by 6 percent and staff turnover increasing to 20 percent, up from just 5 percent two years ago.

Larry was aware of morale problems and decided that an employee survey might help identify what could be done to boost morale, employee engagement, and hopefully solve the quality and turnover problems. The results of the survey provided valuable feedback; however, the management team was shocked and disappointed that the worst scoring area was *trust for management.*

"How can they not trust us?" ranted Larry at the next management team meeting. "Look at the results we have achieved against some pretty stiff competition. They still have their jobs don't they?"

What Larry did not understand was that *being trustworthy* does not guarantee that you will be *trusted*. *Building trust* and *trustworthiness* are two different things. *Trust* is a feeling you have towards someone else. Have you ever *trusted* someone whom you later found out was not *trustworthy*? Have you ever not *trusted* somebody and then, later on, discovered that person was in fact *trustworthy*? Whether you are *trusted* is not just a factor of your *trustworthiness*. It is based primarily on your ability to *build trust*. Leaders must understand the distinction between *building trust* and *being trustworthy*.

Larry did not think about the need to *build trust* with the employees at Nu-Parts. He was too focused on *being trustworthy* to the owners and, in the process, he had in fact seriously diminished *trust* with the employees. Somewhere along the way, his team members became alienated. If things had kept up as they were, many more employees would have left.

To understand the difference between *trustworthiness* and *building trust* and discover what went wrong for Larry, it is necessary to understand the elements that must be present for *trust* to develop.

The **Elements of Trust**™ emerged out of research conducted by one of Integro's founders, Ralph Colby, to determine what needs to be present for trust to develop in a relationship. The **Elements of Trust**™ are:

- **Congruence:** I say what I mean and mean what I say. I walk my talk. I am honest and ethical.
- **Openness:** I am receptive to others' ideas and opinions. I am willing to disclose what's on my mind.
- **Acceptance:** Who you are is OK with me. I do not judge other people.
- **Reliability:** You can count on me to keep my commitments. I do my best at everything I do.

Let's explore each of these a little more closely.

The Elements of Trust ™

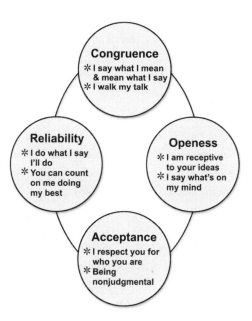

CONGRUENCE

You may remember what congruent triangles are from geometry class. Congruent triangles have angles of the same measure; even though their size may vary, the shape remains consistent. _Congruence_ means the _same as_: what I say is the _same as_ what I really mean. It is walking the talk, or practicing what you preach. _Congruence_ is about principles. Honesty, ethics, and integrity come under the element of _congruence_. It is through your _congruent_ behavior that your team learns about your honesty and integrity.

Congruence can be a tall order, because saying what you really mean is not always what people want to hear. Let's say a female friend of yours buys a dress and models it for you, then asks what you think of it. If you don't like it, or think that it doesn't flatter her, what do you say? Will you be _congruent_ and say what you truly think, which is that the dress looks awful on her? If you say, "_Oh, yeah, it's nice,_" then you almost guarantee her response will be: "_You don't like it, do you?_"

When you are not _congruent_, other people tend to pick up on it. They will see it in your body language, your facial expressions, or in the inconsistency in the tone of your voice. It's a gut feeling that tips us off to how other people are feeling. Sometimes, we feel the need to sugarcoat things or tell white lies so we do not

People can always smell a fish -

53

hurt someone else's feelings. But this can dilute your message as well as diminish the trust the other person has for you now and in the future. Many politicians fail to understand this point. They feed us the information they want us to hear, they do not respond directly to the interviewer's questions, and they expect us not to see through the lack of *congruence*. No wonder so many people are cynical about politics!

OPENNESS

The first President and Founder of Integro, Ron Bates, displayed a sign on the wall above his desk that read: *I can take good news, I can take bad news, but I can't take surprises.* If, as a leader, you discover a change of plans that will affect your employees or you are displeased with their work, then they should be the first to know. If there has been a delay on a delivery, your client should be the first to know. People trust and respect you more for being *open*, even if, and especially if, the news is bad.

No one likes to operate in the dark. Team members want and, in most cases, need to know about their performance and welcome feedback. How *open* are you with the members of your team? Do you encourage them to share their ideas, feelings, concerns, and, most importantly, what they expect of you as their leader? The *openness* you create directly reflects your team's involvement. *Openness* engages people; they want to know more about what is going on. When *openness* is high between you and your team, they are more interested in what the organization does and how well the team and organization are doing. And remember, *openness* is a two-way street.

In some organizations, information is used as power. Unfortunately, some people in upper management often withhold information from people lower down in the organization as a reminder of their power. Team members see this failure to disclose information as a sign: *You don't trust us with this information.* This results not only in a further erosion of trust and engagement, but also leads employees to keep valuable information that could improve the company's performance to themselves. I am not suggesting full disclosure in all matters—some things must remain confidential—but *openness* is vital to your team and your organization's success. When you are more *open* with your frontline team members, they feel more connected to the organization. You cannot build *engagement* and *passion* with people who do not feel connected.

ACCEPTANCE

This is the least obvious of the **Elements of Trust**™, and yet it is the element that allows the other three elements to flourish. When people know they are *accepted* and *respected*, they are willing to be more *open* and are more committed to being *congruent* and *reliable*.

At a seminar a few years ago, I heard a manager say, "When I go to my friend's place to visit with him, I know I can check my ego at the door." This is a great way to look at *acceptance*; when you know that you are truly *accepted* for who you are, you are more likely to say what's on your mind. Can your team members *check their egos at the door* when they are with you? Or do they need to be on guard, wondering when the next judgment or criticism is going to come? Are you a person who believes that *constructive criticism* is good for people?

Constructive criticism is an oxymoron. Criticism cannot be constructive. Criticism is criticism! It is *critical!* The only people I have met who believe *constructive criticism* is positive are those who like to give it. No one really likes to get it. If think you do, what you are really saying is that you welcome *constructive feedback*. It is a semantic difference, I know, but the difference in your team's mind is crucial. When you *criticize* someone, what you are doing is being critical of something that person has done in the past. The past cannot be changed, so dwelling on it is not helpful. What everyone <u>can</u> change is what happens in the future, so it's far more effective to provide someone who has made a mistake with feedback about what has happened, *without criticism*, and then *request* what you would like him or her to do in the future. A good request is focused on the future in terms of ways a person can improve it. People respond more positively to *requests* than they ever will to *criticism*.

When your team members know you *accept* them for who they are, that whatever they say or do is not going to affect how you feel about them as a person, then they know they work in an environment where they can really focus on being the best they can be. I am not saying that you have to *accept* everything someone does. That would be irrational. As a manager in an organization, you do have to evaluate performance and ensure that results are achieved. But you don't have to judge people in a manner that makes them feel inferior in any way. Some managers unconsciously demonstrate a lack of *acceptance* for people by the way they communicate with them, by talking down to them, or by being overly patronizing and condescending. Some managers feel the need to constantly remind people of their own superior experience or qualifications, or they use jargon that they know other people do not understand. These things are not necessarily intended to diminish people, but that is what is achieved.

To become more effective at *acceptance*, you must be more aware of how you communicate with others and be open to feedback as to whether you are creating an environment where people feel *accepted* or not. Until your team members feel you really *accept* them, you will not succeed in building trust, engagement, or passion. Without *acceptance*, you can not reach your own goals.

RELIABILITY

No one wants to work with someone who is unreliable. I'm sure you know from experience that it is hard to have confidence in people who make promises they do not keep. People are quite conscious of whether you are reliable or not. *Can you get the job done?*

Reliability is more than keeping commitments and following through on projects or meeting deadlines. It means committing to those things that you do not necessarily say, but know you must do anyway, like being punctual for meetings. As a leader, it is extremely important to your success that you can *rely* on your team members to deliver the results they are capable of and, in turn, that your team members can expect the same of you.

How often have you been in a meeting where the start time is pushed back, waiting for people to arrive? Are you the cause of these delays? It is not only your *reliability* that suffers when you do that; you are also sending an arrogant message that your time is more important than theirs. It is a lack of *acceptance* as well. Yes, you may be the boss, and what you have to do is really important, but so is what your team members have to do. When you keep them waiting, you diminish their trust. Being *reliable* also means maintaining confidentiality. When people trust you with confidential information of any kind, they expect you to be a vault with it.

Reliability comes in all shapes and degrees. You may be able to *rely* on someone to get a job done, but not to keep confidential information. Some people are always late, but you can completely *rely* on them to do a great job. Just as there are degrees of trust, there are degrees of reliability.

Strengths and Potential Weaknesses

Most people are naturally strong in two of the four **Elements of Trust**™, are competent in a third element, and must work hard on the fourth. Which two of the four elements come most easily to you, and which one takes the most energy? Why don't you pause for a moment and write that down—the two **Elements of Trust**™ that come most easily to you, and the one that takes the most energy.

Some people struggle with being *congruent* because they have difficulty being straightforward with people—they do not want to hurt their feelings or alienate them. On occasion, they may say things they do not really mean to avoid unpleasantness or conflict. Those who are naturally strong in *congruence* do not lack straightforwardness. In fact, they pride themselves on their ability to tell it like it is. Others may see them as blunt or insensitive at times, but you always know where you stand with them.

Some people have difficulty being *open* because they are naturally inclined to be more private. They keep their thoughts and feelings to themselves and require a high level of trust for another person to open up to them, especially about their feelings. Then there are those people who are naturally strong in *openness*, who are happy to share their feelings with anyone who will listen. Sometimes you wish they weren't so open!

People who have difficulty *accepting* are typically less tolerant because they set high standards for themselves and others. When others do not measure up, a short fuse of intolerance ignites; they tend to become critical—whether they express it openly or not. They can also be very self-critical when they do not measure up to their own standards. People who are naturally strong in *acceptance* are more understanding and forgiving of those who make mistakes. It doesn't mean they will *accept* poor performance; they are just more *accepting* of people who are dealing with performance issues.

The primary reason some people struggle with *reliability* is that they tend to over-commit themselves. With the best of intentions, they say they will do something or agree to be at a meeting, but then get overwhelmed with all the things they have committed to and run out of time. These people are often not very time-conscious. They may get so involved in a phone conversation that they completely lose track of time, only to realize later that the meeting started five minutes ago.

Trust Is Not Static

You are either building or diminishing trust all the time. In every relationship you have, everything you do in that relationship, including what you do not do, has an impact on the *level of trust*. It is either going up or down. Understanding this is crucial. You need to be very aware of what you do and the impact your behavior has on the degree to which people trust you. How you behave as a leader is always under the microscope, so you need to be very conscious of whether you are building trust or diminishing it.

You cannot take one element in isolation and expect to build trust. Sometimes you need to deliver bad news or raise an issue you know may hurt someone's feelings. You can be direct, even confrontational, without being unnecessarily harsh on people. You do it by balancing *congruence* with *acceptance*. It is cliché, but it is true to say that honesty is the best policy. Tell the truth, but shape it in a way that helps other people maintain their self-esteem, respect, and dignity. After all, it is how you would like to be treated yourself.

Let's say you have a team member—we'll call him Bill—who is not performing up to his usual standards. He seems distracted at work and his performance is dropping. Here is an example of how you can combine *congruence* and *acceptance* to address this problem:

"Bill, we need to talk, is this a good time?" You want to respect his time and ensure he does not have a major priority on his mind that will distract him. Bill replies that it is a good time for him to talk and you continue: *"Bill, I'm concerned about your work performance of late. I know what you are capable of and you have been a strong contributor to the team, but lately you seem to be distracted. It seems as if your mind is elsewhere and, as a result, your performance has slipped well below your usual standard. Is there a problem?"*

You need to deal directly with the issue and show him you respect and believe in him. Don't tell him what to do because you want him to be *self-directed*. Ask questions to see if he is aware that he has been distracted and his performance is slipping, which encourages a *self-directed* course of action to solve it. Once you've discussed the issue and you both agree that he needs to refocus, ask, *"Well Bill, what do you think you need to do to get back to your usual self? Is there anything I can do to help?"* Another follow-up question could be: *"What can we do to ensure this doesn't happen again?"*

This is an example of *congruent* behavior. If you behave in a *congruent* way, Bill understands that you are being honest with him and that you genuinely care about him. Each of the **Elements of Trust**™ is a behavior. Looking back at the **Whole Person Concept**, it is your behavior that builds trust. Whether you are trustworthy or not is determined by your values or beliefs. When you <u>believe</u> it's important to build trust <u>and</u> be trustworthy, you'll put out the effort to behave in trust-building ways.

Belief in People

Several years ago on an executive coaching assignment in Sydney, I came across one of the worst 360 degree reports I had ever seen. At Integro, we offer a variety of diagnostic tools to assess leadership competencies, one of which is a 360 degree assessment. In a nutshell, the report compares how managers perceive their own leadership competencies against how their team members, peers, and immediate supervisors rate them. Our clients like the 360 degree report because managers who are aware of how their behavior is perceived are better able to adapt and create a *responsibility-based* work environment. In this instance, the manager's team members were, at times, brutal in their assessment of him, particularly in his lack of interpersonal skills. They commented that he had a tendency to micromanage, constantly checking up on employees. This manager rated his own performance very high in every category. The huge discrepancy obviously troubled him.

I met with this manager to debrief his 360 degree report, and ask him to think about whether the results may have something to do with why his staff turnover had increased significantly over the previous year. During the debriefing, he admitted to micromanaging people, so I asked why he felt he had to be so controlling. He said, "To make sure everyone does what they are supposed to do." He operated under the assumption that unless he controlled his team and their situation, they would do the wrong thing!

So I asked, "What do you really believe about the people you've got working for you here?" He thought deeply about his answer for a good thirty seconds in silence, then glanced up at me and said, "I've got some really good people working here." Before the results of the 360 degree report, believing in his people had not really occurred to him. He knew they were trustworthy, but he had not demonstrated this trust. In fact, he had demonstrated the opposite—*a lack of trust!* He also realized he had lost some of his best people because they refused to work for someone who did not trust them.

Control-based approaches are very common in management—too common, I'm afraid. I've said it before and I will say it again: *control-based* management does not achieve the best results. You cannot expect to get the most out of your staff and inspire their passion this way. Too few managers think about whether it is appropriate or what the consequences are for operating in a controlling way. Even *self-directed* people who embrace accountability resent constant surveillance and control by authorities. Ask yourself how you feel when you are being watched and checked on all the time. If you don't like it, why would your team members?

Control-based leaders send a clear message to their staff that they don't trust them to do a good job unless they are controlled. At some point, these managers convince themselves their team's results would be worse if they did not control them. Pretty soon, the most worthwhile employees begin to switch off and stare out the window like bored students in an uninspired class, occasionally glancing at the clock and waiting for it all to be over. If that situation were to continue, you would have resignation letters from most of your best people.

The 360 degree report was the catalyst that convinced this particular manager that his outlook on both leadership and his team was not working for him. Everything I know from personal experience working with many different clients tells me that when employees are asked what they think they can achieve, they set their goals higher than management could have ever set for them. It comes back to that basic decision about whether you believe in people or not.

Do You Believe in Your People?

Trust is the essential foundation for creating a *Responsibility-Based Culture*. When you really trust people, believe in, and partner with them, when you get them more involved and give them more responsibility, then you not only get more *self-directed* behavior from them, but they also become more passionate about what they do. You get people who really want to make a difference.

Take time to think about the people on your team. What are their talents and what do they bring to the table? If you don't know, then it is time to find out. What are the unique strengths of each person? Do they have strengths they could be using that you don't know about?

If you believe in people, you lay the foundation for an open and honest work environment in which employees feel switched on, engaged, and prepared to be passionate about their work. People really do want to make a difference; they want to do their best. Only when you believe this will you be able to build the kind of trusting relationships necessary to get the best performance out of your team and ignite their passion!

GETTING **STARTED** ON **ENGAGEMENT**

The starting point for getting employees engaged is to understand that if their needs are not satisfied, employees switch off.
This section focuses on the people skills leaders need to tune into the different needs and values employees have that will light a fire within each of your team members.

People Skills That Build Trust

My first job after finishing school was for a large insurance company in Brisbane, Australia, working in the commissions department. I was a numbers-cruncher who calculated how much each salesperson made on the policies he or she sold. This was in 1965, so sophisticated equipment like computers and elaborate calculators were not at my disposal, which may or may not have been why I made the mistake of grossly over-compensating a salesperson on a sale he made. The mistake was not caught for some time. When it was, I was called into my manager's office. I trembled as I entered, worried that I would be at least yelled at and contemplating whether I would have my job when he was finished talking to me.

My department manager was a fellow named Alan who was perhaps the best possible manager to introduce me to the world of work. Alan was friendly, made an effort to get to know me, and told me his door was always open if I had any questions. Most important for me was that Alan actually meant this, which made me respect him immensely. When he told me of the error I made, he neither yelled at me nor took my job away. Instead, he pulled out the worksheets for that sale, calmly and rationally showed me the paperwork, and helped me discover where I made the mistake. There were no recriminations, just a focus on making sure I understood where in the process I went wrong so I would not repeat the mistake. What could have been a really bad experience turned into a very positive one. I refocused on my work from then on, making sure everything was perfect, not because I was afraid of making mistakes, but because I wanted to do my best for Alan. I had no plans of letting him down again.

Alan was a prime example of a manager who used all four **Elements of Trust**™ effectively. It is one thing to say you want a high level of trust with your team but quite another to have the patience to actually build it.

Building Trust is just one of four *people skills* needed to be effective as a leader; however, it is a prerequisite—you will not be effective in the other three *people skills* if you have not first *built trust* with your team. That is why I devoted an entire chapter to this foundational people skill. Now, let us focus in on the other three *people skills*: *solving problems, facilitating change*, and *satisfying needs*.

SOLVING PEOPLE PROBLEMS

When problems arise at work, what is the first thing you do? I'm not referring to analytical problem solving techniques; rather, I want you to think about how you deal with your team members when problems arise. Do you immediately ask who caused it and look for the person or persons to blame? Any time you spend on *blame-assigning*, focusing on <u>whom</u> rather than <u>what</u> or <u>how</u>, is time not spent on solving the problem. Have you ever worked for a manager who was a *blame assigner* rather than a *problem solver?* What kind of manager are you?

Unless it is an emergency, the first thing to do when you become aware of a problem is gather information. Then, define what the real problem is and the sequence of events that led up to it <u>before</u> attempting to determine a solution. Gathering information usually means getting input from the other people involved, so they can provide any information they have regarding the steps you need to take to solve it. When addressing the problem, always focus on the *process* that led to the problem, <u>not</u> the *people*.

When Alan became aware of the problem I had caused with my error in calculating the sales commission, he gathered together the information he needed to solve the problem and ensure that I learned from the mistake. When someone makes a mistake, your goal is to determine what needs to be changed to ensure the problem is solved and will not arise again. Getting people to tell you what they know about the problem is the key to being a successful *problem solver* and cannot happen without a high level of trust.

Have you ever had a situation where nobody seems to know anything about the problem but your gut feeling tells you they know more than they are letting on? It reminds me of Sergeant Schultz on the TV series *Hogan's Heroes*, who frequently said, "I know nuttink!" when in fact, he knew exactly what was going on. To successfully gather the information you need, people have to be *open* and *straightforward* with you. That is why the skill of *building trust* must come first; the higher the trust you have with your team members, the more quickly problems are disclosed, and you can immediately get to work on identifying what the real problem is and coming up with the best solution.

Assigning blame achieves the opposite. Witch hunts never work. They put people on the defensive and people become more self-protective by keeping valuable information to themselves. In the future, any information that could incriminate themselves or their co-workers will be withheld. If your employees believe their mistakes will be treated like crimes, they not only try to cover them up, they also stop using any creativity or initiative that might result in mistakes.

FACILITATING CHANGE

I remember a case when a CEO of a manufacturing company with about 100 employees wanted to reward his employees for a good year by introducing a profit-sharing plan. This was a non-unionized plant, so the CEO created a task team of frontline workers to gather input from the rest of the employees and negotiate an agreement. To the CEO's surprise, the workers rejected the profit-sharing plan because they believed management had an ulterior motive and were skeptical of it. The employees just didn't trust management.

In a low-trust workplace, employees will resist change, even when it is beneficial to them.

Most organizations implement change from the top down: the senior management team identifies a problem, decides on the best solution, and implements it, often without any consultation with the employees who will have to make the changes. Do the changes that were made make sense? In this case, the management team said yes. But if employees do not understand the reason for the change, or they have not had the opportunity to contribute to the problem-solving process, they will resist it.

When there is a high level of trust at all levels of the organization, employees are far more receptive to changes being implemented. If employees have been involved in providing input toward defining problems and coming up with solutions, they are more supportive of making the implementation a success. Organizations experiencing a lot of internal resistance to change have not focused enough on the first two *people skills* of *building trust* and *problem solving*. They jump straight to *implementing* change rather than *facilitating* it.

Note that "facilitating change," not "implementing change," is the *people skill* here. This distinction is critical. Think of the typical response people in your organization have toward change when they are not consulted. If your organization is like most, then the reaction is resistance! That was how the manufacturing workers responded when offered a profit-sharing plan.

Here is another example: One of the changes Carol Scott, President of AAA South Jersey, made in her own management approach was to seek input from employees on the organization's strategic plan. In the past, the senior management team had developed the plan and simply announced it. So when George Miller, an accountant and internal auditor, and Penny Tarde, a revenue analyst in member services, were invited to be part of a task team to review the strategic plan before implementation, they were surprised and honored. Neither had been asked to make recommendations to management at this strategic level before.

The task team felt that the strategic plan needed to be more innovative if AAA was to keep pace with new services and an increasing number of members making their own travel bookings online. The task team also came up with a number of new ideas for services that would generate more revenue. They put together a report and presented it to senior executives. The management team embraced and implemented virtually all of their recommendations, greatly contributing to the South Jersey Club having one of its best years ever.

Both George and Penny reported it was a very rewarding experience, and that the ongoing opportunity to participate in town hall meetings and other task teams has made their jobs much more interesting. Penny said, "Even though my job hasn't changed, I enjoy coming to work so much more now."

Facilitating change is a skill that does not come naturally—it has to be learned. It requires you to get team members involved in the change process, not make them victims of it. When they do get involved, they not only embrace change, they enthusiastically help you to implement it because they understand the reason for the change, it makes sense, and they have part ownership in the decision. Your organization reaps the benefits.

SATISFYING NEEDS

How much fun are you to work for? Think about that. You may not have placed much importance on ensuring that your team members enjoy working for you, but if people don't, they won't be passionate about their work either. Having fun at work does not mean throwing a party or having to entertain people. People enjoy working for managers who trust them, believe in them, and really listen to them. People have fun when they are doing something they really like to do and they're good at doing. Leaders can foster that feeling by identifying team members' talents, and ensuring they have the opportunity to use them every day.

Think about your favorite sport while you were growing up. For me, it was track, particularly sprinting and hurdles, as well as rugby. I liked these sports for the same reasons you liked yours—they were the sports I was best at and did well in. By identifying your team members' strengths and making sure they are able to use them, you make important inroads to helping them have more fun at work. Your role is not unlike a coach whose goal is to get the most out of the talents of each team member. People enjoy challenges, though not to the extent that it stresses them out. Challenge them so that they get enjoyment out of the achievement. Overcoming obstacles, solving problems, stretching their minds, having new experiences, and learning how to better utilize strengths are other ways people can have fun at work. At the same time, this improves their contribution to your organization. It is a win-win scenario.

Intrinsic vs. Extrinsic Needs

Research from the Saratoga Institute may explain why many managers fail to satisfy their employees' needs. Leigh Branham, author of **The 7 Hidden Reasons Employees Leave**, reports that "89% of managers believe that employees leave the organization for reasons related to money, according to an article quoted in the Harvard Management Update by Marie Gendron, June, 1998. The Saratoga Institute research shows that 88% of already-departed employees say it was for reasons other than money." The Saratoga survey was conducted in exit interviews with 19,700 employees in 17 different industries from 1998-2003.[7]

If you believe that people are primarily motivated by money, you are at risk of not only having a costly workforce, but also one that is not at all passionate about what they do. Understanding the difference between *extrinsic* and *intrinsic* rewards is the key to igniting the passion in your team. *Extrinsic motivators* are those that come externally to you. For example, a bonus, a pay rise, a promotion, or some kind of reward would be an *extrinsic motivator*. *Intrinsic motivators* are internal, such as seeing what you do as stimulating, interesting, challenging, rewarding, and/or meaningful. There are many ways to satisfy people's needs *intrinsically* that don't cost a cent.

Michelle Poole is a manager with the Department of Social Services in Alamance County, North Carolina. She realized after learning these people skills that she really did not know what her employees needed. Why? She hadn't asked. When she finally did, she learned that one of her team members was not finding satisfaction in her work; specifically, this team member wanted more responsibility and to learn more about other areas of the organization. This surprised Michelle and is something many managers would not expect, especially if they believe that people want to do the least they can get away with. Michelle created the opportunity for this employee to learn about other areas of the agency and, as a result, she took on additional responsibilities and became a much more productive and motivated employee.

Susan Osborne, Director of this agency, says, "Once we created a *Responsibility-Based Culture* in our agency, our child support unit significantly improved retention and exceeded their financial goals for the year. The return on investment for us is measured by how we change the lives of those we serve. When I look at where we were and the process we went through to increase trust and personal responsibility, we are now better able to serve families and make a positive difference in their lives. That's the bottom line for us; we are changing peoples' lives, for the right reasons and in the right way."

Have you asked your team members what would make work more satisfying for them? An even more probing question is: "*What barriers do we need to overcome to make this a great place to work?*" When posing this question to your team, do it in a small group so they can discuss the question and what needs to be done to overcome these barriers. People are more open in small groups, but make sure you are willing to take the feedback. Your leadership approach may be part of the problem that led to the barrier, so there may be times when you have to bite your tongue and just listen. Don't let that same problem get in the way of a solution!

Put Your People Skills into Practice

Take one of the barriers your team sees to creating a great workplace. If a team member says, "*We don't have any input into decisions that affect us,*" then that is an indication that they see this as a *problem*! Don't get defensive. Remember, the problem-solving process begins with gathering information. When you get defensive, you assign blame, often to absolve yourself by making excuses or qualifying their input. If you say it was not your fault, you imply that it was someone else's fault. If input into decisions is a problem with your team, ask team members for examples of decisions where they believe their input would have improved the situation, then inquire how this barrier can be removed in the future. Through discussion, you determine with the team what the best solution is and what needs to be done to *facilitate change*. It is not necessarily all up to you. What can the team do to ensure that the change takes place? Ask them. Once you have got the information, follow through and identify situations where the team can have input and *satisfy the need*. Once the need is met, trust has grown and you are at a new level with your team, a level where the team will be more open with you about what can be done to improve the work environment and their work performance.

Remember, you need all four *people skills* to build trust. To effectively develop these *people skills* in your behavior, you must understand what aspect of you is involved when performing each skill. I'm talking about the four aspects of a person we talked about earlier in the **Whole Person Concept**.

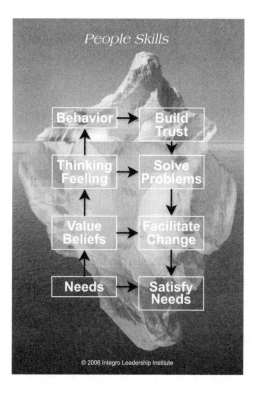

BEHAVIOR

Can you think of a time when someone completely misinterpreted something you said or did? It's happened to all of us more than once. When people only see the tip of your iceberg, they can't see your intentions. Through what is below their own water line, they interpret or project what you do and say through their own filters. *Behavior* is the result of what goes on under the waterline. When people *behave* differently, it is because of what is going on inside them.

Your *behavior* is the aspect of you that performs the skill of *building trust.* (Note the arrow going to the right in the diagram above). What counts is what you do, not what you say you are going to do. If you say you are going to be somewhere at a certain time to meet a friend and you are not there when he turns up, he does not know anything about your intentions or what has happened. The only information he has is that you said you would be there but you are not, and *trust* is diminished. To be effective at *building trust* and creating a great work environment, you must be very aware of how you are *behaving* and the impact your *behavior* is having on the members of your team.

THINKING AND FEELING

Thinking and *feeling* are often in conflict and require some conscious effort to manage. You *feel* like telling a co-worker what you really think of her, but you *think* that could be a career-limiting move. You *feel* like eating that bar of chocolate, but you *think* that you may put on a couple of pounds if you do. Being consciously aware of what you are *thinking* and *feeling* when you are solving problems is an important skill to learn. There are times when it is the right decision to do what you *think* you should do, and other times when it would be more appropriate to go with your gut *feelings*.

It is the *thinking and feeling* aspect that you use when you are *solving problems*. While you are gathering information, you are analyzing that information and thinking through all your knowledge, experience, and technical expertise to arrive at the best solution. You also use judgment and *emotional intelligence*. So both *thinking* and *feeling* come into play when you are in *problem-solving* mode. The more aware you are of your *thoughts* and *feelings*, the better your decision making will be.

VALUES AND BELIEFS

When I joined the Royal Australian Air Force in 1966 to become a navigator, I not only had to learn to navigate airplanes from point A to point B, I had to learn how to become an Officer and Gentleman! As Officer Cadets, we ate in the Officers' Mess, where we learned what all the knives, forks, and spoons were for and other rules of etiquette. One thing that sticks out in my memory is that we were told there were three subjects that were not to be discussed in the bar area: sex, religion, and politics. The obvious reason is that these are subjects people tend to have very personal values about, and therefore strong beliefs. Add some alcohol to the mix which loosens up one's inhibitions and these subjects have the potential to escalate into heated arguments if not a fistfight. That was the theory.

Once I graduated from Navigation School and went to my first squadron, I don't recall anyone holding back on talking about those subjects, or any fistfights breaking out.

The more important a *value* or *belief* is to you, the more passionately you will defend it. Have you been in any intense discussions lately where you passionately *believed* you were right, and the other person thought you were wrong? When you ask people to change the way they do something or what they *believe*, you are in fact saying "*this way is better than your way*" or "*this is right, you are wrong.*" No wonder people resist change, especially if that change feels like an attack on a strong personal *belief*. You are addressing a much deeper level inside a person now than just what they are *thinking*.

If you are going to be effective at *facilitating change* as a leader, then you must understand people will struggle with accepting this new approach, system, method, or product until they *believe* it is better than what they've been doing. You need to be effective at helping people reexamine *beliefs* by *asking questions* that get them thinking about their *beliefs* and considering alternatives. Chapter 9 will focus on the skills needed to develop these questions.

NEEDS

I was early for an appointment with a client a while back in Sydney, so I thought I'd use the time to my advantage and head over to browse at a Mazda dealership for a new car for my wife. I knew what I was looking for, so I went over to a Mazda 323. The salesman approached me and asked, "Are you interested in the 323?" As soon as I said yes, he began his spiel about performance and handling, but that was not why I was interested in this car. I was looking for a car for my wife that was easy to park and had a hatchback and four doors for easy access to the baby seat. Performance and handling was not particularly going to interest my wife at that point in time. But the salesperson was so focused on his own *needs* and what he liked about the car that he made assumptions about my *needs* and ended up way off the mark.

Have you had a similar experience? When you assume you know what others *need*, they may often wonder what you are talking about. You may be attempting to satisfy a *need* that has nothing to do with them. To be effective as a *needs satisfier*, you must get your own *needs* out of the way to find out what the other person's *needs* are; in fact, by satisfying others' *needs*, your own *needs* are more easily met. As I have said, this is part of the **Give-Get Cycle**. Unfortunately, too many managers focus on their own *needs* or the organization's *needs* at the expense of their team members' *needs*. When team members' *needs* are not met, they switch off, become disengaged, and you have lost the passion of another team member. Most organizations have a high percentage of average performers, and you can achieve successful business results by meeting the organization's *needs* at the expense of employees' *needs*. But what is the cost to the organization? What could be achieved if all employees were passionate about what they do and performing at their best every day? You know the answer.

When you create a work environment where team members enjoy coming to work, find what they do meaningful and challenging, and are able to use their strengths every day, team performance improves and so does the performance of the entire organization.

CHAPTER 5

What Makes You Tick?

It surprises those who know me now that when I was a boy, I had an explosive temper. Until I was eight or nine years old, I easily flew into fits of rage at the slightest provocation, most often because of my older brother, Kevin. He knew which buttons to push and when he did, I could be a dangerous ball of rage. Once, Kevin locked me out of the house after I chased him around the yard, trying to hit him for teasing me. I was so angry at him for locking me out that I punched the glass door so hard it shattered. I was not cut or seriously hurt, but I got into a heap of trouble for breaking the glass. My mother repeatedly told me what a bad-tempered little boy I was, and this was just another example. But as far as I was concerned, I was a really nice person with many friends who liked me. I did not see myself as bad-tempered—it was all my brother's fault! If he hadn't teased me, then I wouldn't have reacted the way I did. I vehemently denied that I had a bad temper and got defensive about it when my mother brought it up.

Breaking the glass door was a wake-up call for me. I realized that I did lose control of my emotions and behavior and that I could be dangerous. In fact, I became quite afraid of what else I might do if I did not learn to control myself. I was not in a position to change that aspect of my behavior until I accepted the fact that I did have a bad temper! Interestingly enough, once I accepted responsibility for my own reactions, my brother's teasing did not have the same effect and he eventually stopped. We have been the best of friends ever since.

How well do you know yourself? Have you ever had someone tell you something about yourself you thought was untrue? When people give you feedback you don't agree with, how do you respond? Do you reject it outright and tell them they don't know what they are talking about? Or are you open to exploring the situation to see whether it may be something you didn't realize about yourself?

I am a very keen golfer and play at least once if not twice a week, weather permitting. I have been a student of the golf swing since taking up the sport and continue to take lessons every few months because I believe my handicap does not reflect my true potential. I know what a good golf swing looks like and what I need to do to improve, but I still feel that I need a coach to watch me hit a few balls on the range to get a sense of what I am doing and where the ball's going. Afterwards, my coach and I go inside and videotape my swing from different angles. When we sit down to watch my swing on the monitor, I immediately see what I do that causes the bad shots, even before my coach says anything. It *felt* like I was doing what I should be doing when I was swinging, but the reality was, I was doing something different. Every successful golfer, even Tiger Woods, has a swing coach. Why? Other people see things in our behavior that we don't see!

In the **Whole Person Concept,** your *self-awareness* is primarily inside of you, below the waterline, and your behavior is on the outside for others to see, at the tip of the iceberg. You are far more aware of what you *think* and *feel* than you can be about your *behavior*. How aware are you of the degree to which your *feelings* impact your *behavior*, especially when you are experiencing emotions such as anxiety, anger, or frustration? How aware are you of your *values* and *beliefs* and the degree to which they impact the decisions you make? The more aware you are about yourself, that *whole person* that is you, the more effective you will be as a leader.

Your behavior as a leader creates the environment in which your team members work. It is this environment that determines how they feel about coming to work and how well they perform while they are there. If you want to succeed at creating an environment where all team members are *passionate* about their work and produce outstanding results, you <u>must</u> be highly competent in *self-awareness*.

Have you ever worked for a manager who lacked *self-awareness* and, as a result, also lacked the ability to manage his or her emotions and behavior? This type of manager is usually unable to cope well with stress, is moody, has a tendency to react defensively to feedback, has a short fuse, and blames others for his or her own reactions. A lack of *self-awareness,* coupled with a lack of ability to manage one's own behavior, results in a manager who fails to listen to ideas that people put forward. Such a manager is overly critical, insensitive, and sometimes aloof and arrogant. These kinds of managers are likely to be more focused on meeting their own needs, often at the expense of the organization's needs. It's not hard to see how managers who lack *self-awareness* can undermine any attempt by the organization to create an environment where employees are passionate about what they do.

I hope you have worked for a manager with high *self-awareness*: one who copes with stress well, accepts feedback without getting defensive, takes responsibility for personal decisions and actions, and is genuinely interested in and believes in your team. This kind of manager operates optimistically, builds trust, and is viewed as trustworthy; he or she is sensitive to the needs and feelings of others and is comfortable letting others take responsibility. This is an *emotionally intelligent* manager. In his book ***Working With Emotional Intelligence***, Daniel Goleman says, "In studying hundreds of companies, it became clear to me that the importance of emotional intelligence increases the higher you go in the organization. On average, close to 90 percent of their success in leadership was attributable to emotional intelligence."[8] The stronger your *emotional intelligence* is, the more successful you will be as a leader.

For those unfamiliar with *emotional intelligence*, I suggest the book ***Primal Leadership*** by Daniel Goleman, Richard Boyatzis, and Annie McKee. The book identifies four emotional competencies that define *emotional intelligence*[9]:

- **Self-Awareness:** Being *aware* of your own needs, values, and emotions and their impact on your decisions and behavior is a prerequisite for the other three competencies. You cannot manage your emotions or behavior if you are not first *aware* of them. I was unable to manage my temper as a child until I was *aware* that I had a temper. One of my basic life principles is: *The truth about myself will set me free.* Until you are willing to face the truth about yourself and the impact of your behavior, you cannot change.

- **Self-Management**: *Self-management* involves keeping your emotional reactions in check and being able to behave appropriately when you experience emotions that could result in destructive behavior. Leaders who are strong in this competency are able to control their reactions so they are appropriate to the current situation, and are able to adapt their behavior when the natural, knee-jerk reaction might be inappropriate. Have you ever felt like yelling at someone at work? Yes, some people frustrate and annoy you, but acting out of your emotions does not increase engagement or passion, and can be a career-limiting move.

- **Social Awareness**: Being in tune with others' feelings and needs is having *empathy*. It does not mean you can feel what they feel, but you can mentally put yourself in their situation and attempt to see things from their perspective. Without an *awareness* of your own needs and feelings, you will not be *aware* of others' needs and feelings. You will be more effective at this competence if you get to know more about what lies below your team members' waterlines. What are their values, beliefs, and needs?

- **Relationship Management**: *Relationship management* is all about the ability to build relationships based on mutual trust and respect. Obviously, you cannot be effective in this competency unless you have developed the other three competencies.

Emotionally intelligent managers create an environment that resonates with employees. They stimulate positive emotions in their team members that bring out their best performances. Managers lacking in *emotional intelligence* bring out the worst in their people because they tend to trigger negative emotions.

Everything in this book relates to these four emotional competencies, but this chapter focuses primarily on *self-awareness* since it is such an important first step.

Self-Awareness Is Constantly Changing

Imagine you are pouring a glass of water and someone photographs the glass when you are only halfway through. Even as you keep pouring and the glass continues to fill with water, this does not change the fact that at the exact moment when the photograph was taken, there was a precise amount of water in the glass. That is your *self-awareness*. At any specific moment, when that camera flashes, you had exactly that much *self-awareness*—no more, no less. Every decision you made in your life and every action you took was done with the exact amount of *self-awareness* you had at that very instant. *Hence we are always only able to do our best*

Have you ever regretted or wished you could reverse a decision you made? Wisdom in hindsight is easy—you now have more water in the glass, to follow the analogy. Your *self-awareness* has changed and you have seen the consequences of your actions, whether they are positive or negative. Every decision you make, in fact every decision you have ever made in your life, helped shape your *self-awareness* to where it is today. There are certainly times in your life when you've said, "*I should have known better!*" Maybe so, but you <u>didn't</u> know better. Your *self-awareness* was exactly where it was when you made that decision. Some people are much too hard on themselves because of their mistakes. To this I say, "*Get over it!*" Dwelling on past mistakes or regrets makes you less aware of the opportunities facing you now. It also makes you less aware of your true strengths and talents.

76

Becoming More Self-Aware

Have you ever said or done something and suddenly realized you acted exactly like your mother or father? Scary, isn't it? And yet how many times have you done that without being aware of it? *Self-awareness* is being conscious of what goes on inside you and how it affects your behavior. Can you remember a situation where you reacted with anger towards someone and just lost it emotionally? At what point in time did you become consciously aware of what you were doing?

I remember when one of my sons, who was fifteen at the time, argued with me and refused to listen to what I was trying to say. He kept on saying, "But Dad...! But Dad...!" I have to admit I just lost it, grabbed him by the shirt collar, and started shaking him. When my consciousness emerged out of the fog and I realized what I was doing, I thought, "He really needs this!" So I gave him a few more shakes!

It is in moments like these, when you react out of emotion, that you <u>can be</u> less effective as a leader, and as a person. I emphasize <u>can be</u> because there are times when acting out of your emotions is very appropriate. If you feel very pleased with someone's performance, it is appropriate to let that person know. If you are very enthusiastic about an idea, it is appropriate to share this enthusiasm. If you are more conscious of how you are feeling at any given time, there are more choices you have over the appropriateness of your reactions.

How aware are you of how you are feeling, and the impact those feelings are having on your behavior? Has there been a time when you were puzzled about the way others reacted to you? They are reacting to what they can see—your behavior, or the tip of the iceberg. The more aware you are, the less puzzling others' reactions will be.

Looking back at what we've already covered in this book, there are a number of ideas or models we have been through that have an impact on *self-awareness*. The **Whole Person Concept**, for example, helped me understand that everything I do is motivated by my *needs* or my *values*. It is filtered through my *thinking* and *feelings* and I will react directly out of that, but it helps me be aware that I have choices about how I behave. I don't have to react to the way I *feel*; I can decide to act a certain way because I *think* I should, even if I *feel* like doing something else. The more aware I am of my *whole person*, the more I can relax and react the way I *feel* when an immediately emotional reaction is appropriate.

The **Personal Responsibility Model** is also a valuable tool for increasing *self-awareness*. I was thirty years old when I first saw this model, and was shocked to realize just how *other-directed* I had been for much of my life. I still rebelled against my father in some ways and it was a real wake-up call for me to realize that when I rebelled, my behavior was still being controlled by my father, the *authority*! I was doing the opposite of what <u>he</u> wanted me to do rather than freely choosing what <u>I</u> wanted to do. The motivation for my behavior was not my own; rather, it was done out of resentment or rebellion. I was *blind* to the fact that I was *other-directed* and, as a result, I thought that the things in my life that weren't working were not my fault. I always had excuses for not achieving more. People who operate in an *other-directed* way are mostly unaware that they are doing it.

The idea that being trustworthy doesn't mean people will trust you is another key concept for increasing *self-awareness*. Being aware that it is *building trust* that determines whether people trust you, not how *trustworthy* you think you are, is also crucial to building trusting relationships. You cannot simply assume that because you are trustworthy, people will trust you, especially if the element of trust they are best at happens to be the one you struggle with.

Understanding Behavior

Do you work with people who are a mystery to you? You wonder why they do the things they do because it doesn't make sense to you. As you know from the **Whole Person Concept,** that behavior reflects what is going on below their waterline. The key to understanding behavior is to understand what drives it. You don't need to be a psychologist to understand the two basic needs that influence how people behave in relation to each other. *need for affiliation* and *need for control.*

THE NEED FOR AFFILIATION

When you first meet someone, do you tend to be friendly and open, or are you more likely to keep your feelings to yourself? Everyone has a need to *affiliate* with other people to some extent. People with a *high need for affiliation* need to be with people. They are friendly, sociable, and like to talk with others because they care about people. They show their feelings in their facial expressions and tone of voice because of their need to connect with people on a feeling level.

Conversely, there are people with a *low need for affiliation*. They don't need to be around people so much, and when they are, they don't need to connect on a feeling level. As a result, they don't show much feeling in their facial expressions and their tone of voice tends to be more matter-of-fact. They are likely to be more interested in working on a project or task, doing research, or pursuing some form of intellectual pursuit and generally tend to *detach* from people to do it. If they don't *detach* physically, they will *detach* mentally and emotionally to focus on their own priorities.

There is neither a good nor bad, a right nor wrong level of *need for affiliation*. People are just different. Some have a *high need for affiliation*, some have a *low need*, and still others may fall somewhere in the middle of the scale. Problems caused by the differences between people on this dimension occur when we expect people to be like us. If you have a *high need for affiliation*, you want to affiliate, so you expect other people to be friendly towards you. When a person with a *low need for affiliation* is not friendly towards you, or does not want to engage in conversation because he or she is busy, you may judge that person as *antisocial*, or worse, as a person you can't trust.

It is just as OK to have a *low need for affiliation* as it is to have a *high need!* Being *aware* of your own level of *need for affiliation* and being able to adapt to where others are is more important than where you are on the scale.

THE NEED FOR CONTROL

The other factor coming into play whenever two or more people get together is the *need for control*. If you have a *high need for control*, you prefer to take control and like being in charge of projects. You enjoy guiding and directing, making decisions, taking the lead, encouraging, supporting, protecting, and teaching others. If you have a *low need for control,* you are comfortable *adapting* to those who are in control. You may prefer to do the work yourself rather than take charge of others who are doing the work. You have a need to trust the people who take control so you can have confidence in the direction and guidance they provide.

Again, there is no good or bad, no right or wrong. It is perfectly OK to have a *high need for control* and to have a *low need for control.* We just need to be careful not to judge others who are different. For some reason, people with a *high need for control* often view themselves as superior, and yet they could not have achieved anything without the support of those who allowed them to take control. People with a *low need for control* are content to say, *"No, I don't want to be in control. Let them have it."*

We'll talk more about the importance of *behavioral adaptability* later, but for now I want to emphasize that just because you have a need does not mean you have the right to satisfy it *all the time!* Having a *high need for control* does not mean that you have a right to be in control all the time, or that you will be effective if you are in charge. Having a *low need for affiliation* does not mean that you should not attempt to be friendly to someone who has a *high need for affiliation*.

Interpersonal Theory

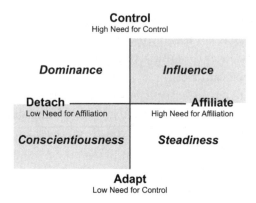

The DiSC® Behavioral Model

When these two dimensions of *affiliation* and *control* are combined and placed at right angles to each other (see the Interpersonal Theory graphic), we have four basic behavioral styles. The next chapter goes into an in-depth understanding of each of the four behavioral styles, but here is an overview of the **DiSC®** dimensions:

- **Dominance**, or the D dimension: People strong in this dimension have a *high need for control* and a *low need for affiliation*. As a result, they are direct and decisive and like being more task-oriented, taking control of projects and tasks, and organizing them. They prefer to have others do the detail work.

- **Influence**, or the I dimension: People strong in this dimension have a *high need for control* and a *high need for affiliation*. While they also want to be in control, their focus is on influencing and persuading people. Because of their enthusiasm and optimism, they get people moving. They also prefer to have others to do the detail work.

- **Steadiness**, or the S dimension: People strong in this dimension have a *low need for control* and a *high need for affiliation*. They are friendly, helpful, and supportive and they genuinely care about people and get satisfaction from doing things for others. Supportiveness is another "S" word that I think is a good fit for this style.
- **Conscientiousness**, or the C dimension: People strong in this dimension have a *low need for control* and a *low need for affiliation*. As a result, they tend to have a preference for doing tasks themselves rather than taking charge or working closely with others. They are focused on quality and accuracy, making sure the task is done right the first time.

The **DiSC˚ Model** describes behaviors that are easily recognizable in people. Since your behavior creates the environment your team members work in, it makes more sense in this context to address behavioral style rather than personality or psychological type. I also think it makes sense for you to take a **DiSC˚** profile so that you have an accurate awareness of your behavioral style. For information about how to take this profile online, see the last page of this book.

Why Use DiSC®?

Because **DiSC˚** is a behavioral model, it describes that aspect of the **Whole Person Concept** that you are least aware of in yourself and most aware of in other people. To understand the environment you create as a leader, you need to understand how your behavior is perceived.

Because the only aspect of what you can see in others is the tip of the iceberg—their behavior—you cannot see what is going on below the surface, especially with people who keep their feelings to themselves. *Passion* is below this waterline. The decision to become *passionate* about something is based on what is going on inside people. A good understanding of the **DiSC˚ Model** not only helps you to create a work environment where your team members are more likely to become more *passionate* about their work, it also gives you insight into your team members' individual needs and what you can do to *light a fire* within them.

Being Different Is Not Wrong

You have no doubt been compared to a brother or sister or parent at some time in your life. Maybe it was a teacher comparing you to another student: "*Why aren't you more like Elizabeth (or Johnny)?*" Either way, the message you likely interpreted was that the other person was better than you. Many times when we were growing up, we got the message: *Different = Wrong.* The converse may also be true, that when we are compared to others as an example for good performance or behavior we may also get the message that we were *better than* other people. It may have been a while since someone else compared you negatively to another person (I hope it has), but have you now carried over the comparisons to that person? Do you need to see yourself as *better than* other people because you are different from them? Do you compare yourself negatively to others because you are different? Being different doesn't make anyone better than anyone else. It just means *you are different!*

Different = Different

We'll return to this topic of dealing with differences in more depth later. The important point here is this: *different behavioral styles* are neither good nor bad, just different. Each style has its strengths and its limitations. Each style has needs and fears. In the next chapter, we'll delve into those differences in depth so that you have a much better idea of how to recognize the differences and diagnose what it takes to *light a fire* within each of your team members.

Why People Do What They Do

Diana, a Human Resources Director, was participating in a train-the-trainer seminar to learn how to apply **DiSC°** in her organization when she recalled a recent work situation. Diana, who happened to be strongest in the *Influencing* dimension, is naturally friendly, outgoing, and enthusiastic and with her *high need for affiliation*, enjoys being with people. Diana had just hired a new administrative assistant named Barbara.

Diana saw Barbara sitting alone at a table in the crowded company cafeteria on her first day at work. Barbara appeared shy and reserved, so Diana went over and sat with her with the intention of making her feel welcome. She is good at that. So she started asking Barbara questions to get to know her about her family, where she grew up, and what schools she went to. Diana noticed that Barbara was becoming flustered and her face had turned red. Diana said, "What's wrong, Barbara? Are you OK?," but Barbara suddenly got up and rushed out of the cafeteria. Diana was confused. She couldn't figure out what had gone wrong, so she assumed that Barbara must have been feeling ill.

Now weeks later, Diana is attending this seminar to learn about **DiSC°** and, as I was describing that people who are high on the *Conscientiousness* dimension have a high need for privacy, *the penny dropped!* Diana realized that Barbara fit the description of the high *Conscientiousness* style, and that she had totally invaded her space at lunch that day by asking so many personal questions. Diana would have been very comfortable answering the same questions she asked Barbara; she would have felt very welcomed. But not everyone likes what we like. Quite frankly, I like it that way, but it does make it more challenging to be an effective leader.

Diana realized some of her natural behaviors made Barbara very uncomfortable, and that to gain Barbara's trust, she needed to adapt her natural style and respect Barbara's need for privacy. As Barbara began to trust Diana more, she also began to feel more comfortable with Diana's outgoing style, and even started to open up more with her.

As a leader, it is essential for you to value the different behavioral styles of each person in your team if you want everyone to perform at his or her best. You need the natural strengths of all styles to create a *high-performance team*.

Exploring DiSC® in Depth

Understanding the differences between people—why people do what they do—is a very valuable skill. There are ten factors we are going to explore to understand what goes on below the waterline: how each style thinks and feels, what their needs are, how they make decisions, and how all this affects their behavior. We'll first identify the ten factors, and then examine how they apply to the four dimensions of personality.

1. **Initial Impressions**: How to recognize a person's style.
2. **Preferred Work Environment:** The environment each style expects at work.
3. **Security**: What each style needs to feel secure in their environment.
4. **Outstanding Need**: What each style principally *desires* more than anything for fulfillment.
5. **Measures Progress By:** How people of each style are tangibly reminded of how well they are doing.
6. **Major Fears**: What does each style fear the most?
7. **Irritated by:** What annoys each style most about other people?
8. **Making Decisions:** How each style naturally makes decisions.
9. **Major Limitation**: The one thing that can stop each style from being successful. *Please pay special attention!* To overcome your own limitations, you must be aware of them. Otherwise, it will trip you up time and time again. I often see leaders preventing their own success because they cannot master this limitation.
10. **Need to Learn**: What *attitude* and *behavior* do people of each style need to learn to overcome their major limitation?

Now let's focus on each of the four behavioral styles. The numbers correspond to the criteria listed above.

DOMINANCE
High Need for Control/Low Need for Affiliation

1. You will recognize people who are high in *Dominance* by their *high self-confidence, assertiveness, goal orientation, competitiveness* and high *sense of urgency.* This is not to say other styles aren't competitive, just that people high in the D dimension tend to show their competitiveness outwardly, to the extent of being verbally competitive and enjoying getting into debates or arguments.

2. People high in *Dominance* prefer *fast-paced, busy, formal,* task-oriented environments where they can, without the distraction of small talk or socializing, get things done.

3. People high in the *Dominance* dimension feel secure when they are in *control,* and of course, they don't feel secure when someone else is in control. Being in control of their time is particularly important, and as a result, they tend to work to a tight schedule. Everything is planned!

4. The outstanding need for people high in *Dominance* is *achievement.* They're more task-oriented. They set goals, and then achieve them. If they play a sport, then they compete to win. What do they do in their leisure time on weekends? Set goals and *achieve* them. What do they do on vacation? They *achieve* things! *Relaxation* for this style is achieving goals and what they feel most comfortable doing. It may appear that their real motive is power and control, but the underlying reason is that more power and control helps them achieve more!

5. People high in *Dominance* measure their progress by the *results* they achieve. They seek acknowledgement of this achievement in tangible terms (i.e. outcomes, the bottom line, etc.), not by the praise or credit they get from other people. Once they see results it's been there, done that, and on to the next project. This style is easily frustrated, and may appear to be a *troublemaker* if they cannot see the results of their own efforts. They are often resistant to participating in teams for this reason. It is important for this style to be able to measure the results of what they do. If they cannot see results, then they will have no *passion!*

6. Although their outstanding need is for *achievement,* a person high in *Dominance* does not fear failure: their major fear is the *loss of control.* As risk-takers, their failure or mistakes are not that big a deal. If they fail, they'll try something else. However if they're *not in control* or others are trying to *take advantage of them,* their ability to achieve their goals is threatened. They may see you as the enemy, trying to undermine their achievements. This is the primary reason why many managers over-control or micro-manage people.

They believe that if they don't control everything and are not watching people all the time, employees will take advantage of them and they won't get results. No wonder they set up an adversarial relationship with their employees: *They see them as the enemy!*

7. People high in *Dominance* are irritated by *inefficiency, indecisiveness* and *slowness*. Who would these people see as being most *inefficient, indecisive* and *slow*? A good first guess would be those high on *Steadiness*—the style directly opposite the D. It makes sense because of their differences in styles, but in reality people high in *Dominance* may see anyone else who is not high in *Dominance* as *inefficient, indecisive*, and *slow*. If this describes you, the reason these things irritate you is because of your outstanding need for *achievement*, and your natural *sense of urgency*. You want results quickly! When others are *inefficient, indecisive* or *slow*, at an unconscious level you believe these behaviors will limit your ability to *achieve results*. The fear of *losing control* kicks in, and you react. The key to dealing with these situations more appropriately is to first recognize them when they arise as *teachable moments*, it is an opportunity for you to learn to be more effective. Second, you need to think about why this person behaves as they do. The **DiSC** model puts you in a better position to understand why people are behaving the way they are, and you will be able to respond more appropriately.

8. People high in the *Dominance* dimension tend to make *quick* decisions because of their high sense of urgency. They are results-oriented, so if there is a decision to be made, they will quickly sum up the facts, decide, and act. As a result, some of their decisions don't work out well for them because they make mistakes! But they see these failures as experiments rather than mistakes. *OK, so that didn't work, let's try something else!* It is not necessarily reckless, but they are, by nature, risk-takers and are *action-oriented*. They learn from their mistakes and make another decision—quickly!

9. The major limitation for people who are high in *Dominance* is *impatience*. In fact, they view their *impatience* as a strength. They have a *high sense of urgency*, make quick decisions, and they get things done. However, because of their impatience, they tend not to listen to what others have to say, especially others whom they see as *inefficient, indecisive,* and *slow*. Because of their strengths in taking charge, high self-confidence and results-orientation, it is not hard to see how they could come to the conclusion that they are superior to others and therefore be somewhat dismissive of others' ideas. This can be corrosive in the long term as people stop giving them ideas and information that would help them achieve even greater success. They often come across as arrogant and lacking humility, further reinforcing others' belief that it's futile talking to them because they just won't listen.

10. People high in the *Dominance* dimension must learn *humility* if they are going to overcome their limitation of *impatience*. Part of the reason people with this style find themselves in leadership positions is that they are quick decision-makers and self-confident, therefore they are good at achieving results. One of the reasons they tend not to listen to other people is that they don't think their input will be worthwhile. Seeing oneself as superior to others means judging others as inferior or lacking *acceptance* of them. This erodes trust and extinguishes any desire to be engaged. The final result is diminished team performance. Humility recognizes that, *different equals different. Different does not equal better or worse, just different! All people have strengths and weaknesses, and everyone has a different perspective from my own, therefore I need to listen to other people's input.* That is the behavior that the *Dominance* dimension needs to learn, which is to *truly listen!* This requires patience and it lets the other person know their input is worthwhile.

INFLUENCE
High Need for Control/High Need for Affiliation

1. People high in the *Influence* dimension can be identified as talkative, filled with enthusiasm, optimism, energy, and they often have vivid imaginations. They have many ideas and feel a need to share those ideas with as many people as possible in order to garner support. They neither hide nor spare their feelings and tend to be very expressive with their tone of voice, their facial expressions and in their mannerisms.

2. They also prefer a fast-paced work environment, but expect it to be *stimulating*, *personal*, and *friendly*, where there are many opportunities for interaction with others.

3. Security for people high in the *Influence* dimension is created when there is a high level of flexibility; when they don't feel boxed in, and where there is an opportunity for variety. As a result, they tend to resist working to a fixed schedule, so time management can be quite a challenge for them. The key is to schedule *responding time* in their day in addition to the tasks that must be done. They are going to respond to people spontaneously, so why not allow for it?

4. People high in the *Influence* dimension have an outstanding need for *social recognition*, to be highly visible, respected, and well regarded by others. Their high need for both control and affiliation drive them to be in leadership roles, but with a focus on *gaining the support of others* rather than controlling them. They have a need to use their ideas to *influence* people and enjoy the respect they get from others as a result.

5. Because of their need for recognition, the *Influencing* style measures their progress by the amount of *praise* or *applause* they get. Getting an email that they have done a great job is nice, but for this style, being told in front of the whole team is significantly more inspiring. In the work environment, this style understands that they don't get much recognition unless they achieve something, so they are usually very focused on achieving results as well. But unlike those high on Dominance, once they achieve the goal they will be looking for the *applause* or *praise*. If it doesn't come, they feel unappreciated. If they fail to get the credit they deserve, the fire within them will be extinguished.

6. For the *Influence* dimension, the primary fear is the *loss of influence*. Their need for *recognition* can only be met when they have influence. This fear can result in the leader who is strong in the "i" dimension wanting to lead all the time because they feel as soon as they stop being the leader, their *influence* will cease. Being ignored or not listening to their ideas will also stimulate this fear.

7. People high in the *Influence* dimension are irritated by *routine* and *formality*. They love *variety* and like to do things differently. They'll take a different route on the way to work, or catch a different train just for a change. They'll experiment with doing their work differently because they loathe boredom and tediousness. Because this style tends to be a casual, informal kind of person, formal protocol like filling out unnecessary paperwork to get approval for something irritates them. They prefer to deal with people on a first name basis. They unconsciously see formality as limiting their freedom and spontaneity—as unnecessary rules others have created to control them. It is not uncommon to see people high in *Influence* resent routine, even rebel against it and do their own thing. If this describes you, you need to learn to recognize the situations when you do tend to *resent* or *resist*, and choose the *self-directed* course of action. This means you need to *agree* to do it, or *disagree*, if that is appropriate. If you disagree, you need to let others involved know what you are doing, and the reason why you don't agree. Then you need to be prepared to *accept the consequences* of your decision.

8. People strong in the *Influence* dimension are also fast-paced, but they tend to trust their feelings and intuition more, so their decisions are more *spontaneous*. They can be compulsive shoppers when they see something and their gut feeling says: *I have to have it.* Although it is feeling that drives their decisions, they are very good at retrospectively justifying that decision with logic. Like those who are high in Dominance, they are less concerned with making a *wrong decision*. It *felt* right at the time and if it didn't work out they can always make another decision.

9. The major limitation of the *Influence* dimension is a *lack of follow-through.* Again, we can best understand this limitation by looking at their strengths of *enthusiasm, optimism,* and *energy.* If you have these strengths, you will be good at getting things started. If you want to get a project moving, you need someone with *enthusiasm, optimism,* and *energy* from the outset. But, when the project gets into maintenance mode, you need strengths of *persistence, patience,* and *attention to detail* to follow through and finish the project. They're strengths don't apply at that stage of the project, so what they typically do is lose interest and start another project. After all, that's what they are good at. Another challenge for people high in the "i" dimension is their tendency to *over commit* themselves, and run out of time to do everything. Again, it is their strengths that leads to them over-committing. They just have so much enthusiasm and energy, thinking *of course I can do it.* Unfortunately, far too often they fall short of what they committed to do.

10. The attitude the *Influence* dimension needs to learn to overcome their lack of follow-through is *self-discipline.* Because they get carried away with their *enthusiasm, optimism,* and *energy,* they can lose touch with reality. When they are involved in an interesting conversation or when they are doing something about which they are passionate, they can be oblivious of the time. The *behavior* they need to learn is to *stop and think,* perhaps count to ten, before making a commitment to do something or leaving a task to go on to another one. Because they are so spontaneous, they need to ask themselves: *What are the consequences of doing this? ...* before they do it! I've found that setting alarms works well for those high in the "i" dimension to remind them of their commitments—but set these alarms to allow enough time for preparation or unforeseen challenges. For example, because of their optimism, people with this style expect that all the traffic lights will be green on their way to a meeting. That may happen one in a hundred times, so allow for some red lights. If a meeting starts at 10:00 a.m. and it takes you five minutes to get there, then start preparing for what you need to take to the meeting at 9:30, not at 9:55 while you are walking to the meeting. In fact you better leave for the meeting at 9:45 because you are sure to run into someone you know on the way. You'll just *have* to stop for a chat! Every computer and personal organizer has an alarm system. Learn to use it.

STEADINESS
Low Need for Control/High Need for Affiliation

1. You'll notice *calmness* and *patience* in people high in the *Steadiness* dimension. They are *cooperative* and *friendly*, although because they are more subdued, their friendliness is more low-key than the effervescence of the "i" dimension. You may need to pay closer attention to their mannerisms to see their friendliness, until you get to know them. *Persistence* is another one of their strengths.

2. People high in *Steadiness* prefer a *slower-paced* environment that is *team-oriented* and *friendly*. They want to be busy, but without the pressure and sense of urgency those high on Dominance tend to create. Harmony is also important to them.

3. The *Steadiness* style feels secure when they're in *close relationships*. They may be slow to make a friend, but, once they have, they will be loyal to that friendship. Since it does take time to build close relationships, it is important to invest that time with new people on your team who are strong in this dimension.

4. The outstanding need for the *Steadiness* dimension is *acceptance*. They satisfy this need for *acceptance* by *giving support* to others. They often unselfishly do things for others without being asked, expecting nothing in return. *Stability* is also an important need for people high on *Steadiness*, especially when it comes to relationships.

5. People high in *Steadiness* are a low key, more reserved "people-person" than the *Influence* dimension so their feedback needs to be low key. They seek *appreciation*, not applause, and may feel embarrassed if your feedback is too over-the-top in praise of them. People high on the S dimension do not give help and support because they are consciously thinking about the *appreciation* they'll get. They sincerely care about people, and want to be helpful. Their fire is stoked when they get genuine, sincere and appropriate *appreciation,* but you have to really mean what you say.

6. People high on the *Steadiness* dimension most fear *disappointing others*. Because of their outstanding need for *acceptance,* they are concerned about how other people feel about them. Because they genuinely care about people, they fear they will in some way let others down or hurt their feelings. This fear can paralyze a manager. If they base their decisions on consensus because they want everyone to be happy, but only some team members agree on what that decision should be, then they're stuck! Because of this fear, this style can have difficulty giving straight answers to questions because they don't want to dis-

appoint anyone. You need to take these things into consideration when you have people high in *Steadiness* on your team. Pushing them to make quicker decisions or asking them to *just get to the point!* increases their fear, and could result in them being even more indirect and, worse still, less engaged.

7. The *Steadiness* dimension is irritated by *insensitivity* and *impatience*. Because they care for and are focused on supporting others, they are most irritated by people who are *insensitive* toward and *impatient* with people. *Patience* is among the S dimension's strengths, so they find it troubling to understand how anyone can be so *unaware* of others' feelings. If this description is you, be careful you don't become guilty of the very things you find irritating in others, *insensitivity* and *impatience*. Remember, they don't see the world or the people in it through the same filters you do. Be *sensitive* to their need to achieve results and *patient* with them in helping them understand what your needs are. If you judge them as being Not OK, you can be sure their *insensitivity* and *impatience* towards you will increase.

8. The *Steadiness* dimension, like the "i" dimension, relies a lot on feelings in *making decisions*, but in their case it has more to do with having *empathy* for others who may be affected by their decision. They are *considerate* decision makers and, as a result, they take more time to make decisions. They need input from others to *consider* how the decision might impact them. This is a good approach until they get conflicting input. There comes a time when the right decision must be made regardless of how everyone feels about it.

9. The *Steadiness* dimension's major limitation is to be *overly modest*. Their strengths of *persistence, patience,* and *procedure-orientation* make them really good at supporting others in achieving their goals. They can be so focused on other people's goals that they see their own strengths as having less value than the strengths of others. They also tend to be concerned about how others perceive them because of their outstanding need for *acceptance*. This can lead to them being very self-conscious, even self-effacing, which makes accepting compliments difficult.

10. People high in the *Steadiness* dimension need to learn the attitude of *self-determination:* to be determined to take care of their own needs and develop a stronger belief in themselves. Behavioral style is not an indication of a person's worth. Everyone, regardless of their behavioral style has strengths and limitations. People who are strong in the *Steadiness* dimension need to pay even more attention to acknowledging their strengths, and recognize that they have as much to contribute to the organization as anyone else does. Their strengths in *getting things done, building and maintaining relationships, increasing customer satisfaction,* and *loyalty* are indispensable to any organization.

These strengths are often not valued as much by some people, but that does not mean they are not equal in value to the strengths of others. The behavior people High in the S dimension must learn is to *set and achieve their own goals*. They can be so focused on meeting their need for *acceptance* by helping others to achieve goals that they neglect to establish goals for themselves. Their goal becomes helping others, and unfortunately, some people will take advantage of that.

CONSCIENTIOUSNESS
Low Need for Control/Low Need for Affiliation

1. What you may notice first about people high in the *Conscientiousness* dimension is their concern for *accuracy* and *high standards*. They have an *analytical* mind, an eye for *detail*, and typically enjoy solving problems. They usually keep their feelings to themselves, which can make it more difficult to get to know them. They are more *cautious* in answering questions and communicating information because they need to think through what they say and make sure it is accurate before they say it.

2. The *Conscientiousness* style prefers a *structured, organized, functional* work environment. They want a quiet, formal workplace, where there are no distractions, allowing them to focus on achieving their high standards of quality and accuracy.

3. People high in the "C" dimension need *preparation* to feel secure. They can't ensure accuracy and high standards without time to prepare, especially when required to do a formal presentation. They need to have enough time to make sure everything will go perfectly.

4. People high in *Conscientiousness* have an outstanding need for *correctness*. Especially important to them are the high standards they must achieve when they take sole responsibility for a task. People high in this dimension also have a strong need for *privacy*. They need to be able to concentrate on their project —so don't invade their personal space like Diana initially did with Barbara.

5. The *Conscientiousness* dimension measures their progress by *being right*. Not only *getting things right*, but also *doing the right thing!* They not only want to meet their high standards for *quality* and *accuracy*, they also want to make sure they are playing by the rules. They want to know what the policies and procedures are so they can stick to them. Like those who are high in Dominance, the feedback this style looks for comes from the task itself. The *Influence* and *Steadiness* dimensions, by contrast, look for feedback from other people, due to their *high need for affiliation*.

6. The greatest fear for the *Conscientiousness* dimension is to be *criticized for what they do*. They put so much effort into doing the task right the first time. They do all the research and analysis thoroughly because they *need to be right!* Yes, they also fear making mistakes, but to be criticized for it is, to them, the worst thing that could happen. If this is your style as a manager, beware of the temptation to believe that you are always right. You may have the evidence to prove that you are right, but so did the church leaders have evidence that the sun revolved around the earth. There is more than one way to do things. Experiment with new solutions to improve performance or customer satisfaction, knowing that in the process of experimenting you may make mistakes, but don't let your fear of making mistakes kill creativity and innovation.

7. People high in *Conscientiousness* are irritated by *surprises* and *unpredictability.* Remember the saying: *I can take good news, I can take bad news, but I cannot take surprises.* You cannot predict accurate results or produce high-quality output when you are uncertain about your facts or when people are not predictable. Being *surprised* by new information, especially after the completion of work, is extremely irritating to this style. If this describes you, remind yourself when you start to get irritated that some people really thrive on a lack of structure and predictability and don't share your core needs. Striving for total certainty and predictability could kill innovation and bog people down in a mire of rules, policies, and procedures that will have customers, and maybe employees, leaving in droves. Don't let a lack of certainty or predictability hijack your emotions or behavior. When you feel yourself getting anxious, ask yourself: *Do I really have to be certain in this situation?* If you do, *choose* the appropriate course of action, and explain to others why you feel it is essential. If you don't have to be, then learn to *let it go!*

8. Like the Dominance dimension, those high in *Conscientiousness* base their decisions on facts and logic, but they are more *deliberate* than quick in their decision making style. They do their research, gather and analyze information, and *deliberate* over it so they can come to the *right* decision. This style is much more concerned about making mistakes because of their outstanding need for *correctness,* so they tend to put off making a decision until they are *certain* it is *right.* This can lead to *paralysis by analysis* and, in some case, the decision not being made. People with this style must learn to work through the *fear of making mistakes* when making decisions.

9. Because they have such high standards, the *Conscientiousness* dimension's major limitation is to be *overly critical of themselves.* They can also be highly critical of others. However, it is their own *self-criticism* and *self-doubt* that limits them from performing at their best. They expect perfection in everything they do and their eye is well tuned to notice flaws. When they critique what they have done, they tend to look for what is wrong, not what is right. They tend to critique other people's work the same way. If you have ever worked for a manager who was strong in *Conscientiousness* or had a parent with this style, you know what I am talking about. You may have scored 97 percent on the test, but they will be focused on the 3 percent you got wrong. Focusing on the negative produces negative feelings. Criticism, even if it is called *constructive criticism,* is still criticism that results in negative feelings. Negative feelings kill *passion!*

10. The attitude people high in the *Conscientiousness* dimension need to learn is *Self-Acceptance.* Their strengths in *accuracy, attention to detail,* and *producing high quality* are needed in every organization, but when these strengths are taken to extreme, this style becomes *overly critical.* Often, even though they have done a great job, they tear it down because it isn't quite perfect. One example would be of an artist tearing up a canvas—that someone would quite happily have bought and put on the wall—just because there were a couple of imperfect brush strokes. Once people with this style have learned to be more accepting of themselves, they will be more *accepting* of other people. The behavior this style must learn is to experiment with *taking risks.* Their needs for *certainty* and *predictability* limit them from achieving their true potential. If this is you, then give yourself permission to *make a mistake.* Try something different in an area of your work where you can recover from a mistake. If it doesn't work out, learn from it, and move on. Don't start beating up on yourself!

There is one more area of difference between people that is important to understand, but I have left it until last because it is the most important: *What are the strengths and potential limitations of each **DiSC** style in building trust?*

DiSC® and the Elements of Trust™

Here is an example of how trust can break down between trustworthy people just because their behavioral styles are different:

A few years back, I took a senior executive team through a five-day leadership program I had developed, called "Leadership at the Summit." The program included a number of outdoor adventure experiences, one of which was a cross-country navigation exercise where participants had to find their way across difficult terrain, build a rope bridge across a creek, and solve some interesting challenges along the way. To spice up the challenge, I gave each team a bucket of water to carry with them with the instructions that the liquid was their company's secret formula to spill it would be to fail the mission.

At one of the check points along the way, participants were handed personalized envelopes marked "private and confidential." Inside were cards that read: There is a traitor in your group who is going to spill the formula. All the cards said the same thing. It was a test to see how the team handled a challenge to the *trust level* in the team. One group of five executives had two members whose highest **DiSC**° dimension was Dominance, and one each whose highest dimension was Influence, Steadiness, and Conscientiousness. The person who was highest on the "i" dimension immediately upon opening his envelope blurted out, "Mine says there's a traitor in the group. What does your say?" The two high "Ds" and the high "S" quickly confirmed that their cards said the same thing, and everyone turned toward Simon, the person high on "C" (who happened to be carrying the bucket of water at the time), and asked him what his card said. His response, as he put his envelope and card away in his inside jacket pocket was: "I can't tell you!"

One of the managers who was high on "D" immediately yelled, "You're the traitor!" and tried to wrestle the bucket of water away from him. Simon did not let go and, after a short but fruitless struggle, the group reluctantly allowed Simon to continue to carry the bucket, but the rest of the team watched Simon like a hawk for the remainder of the exercise. Though no "formula" was spilled and the team successfully completed the mission, the *trust level* continued to be low as Simon stubbornly refused to let anyone else have the bucket or reveal what was on his card.

To understand what happened in this group, let's look at the strengths and potential limitations of each of the four **DiSC**° dimensions in the context of the **Elements of Trust**™.

DiSC and the Elements of Trust

Dominance	Influence
+ve: *Straightforwardness* -ve: *Acceptance*	+ve: *Openness* -ve: *Reliability*
Conscientiousness	Steadiness
+ve: *Reliability* -ve: *Openness*	+ve: *Acceptance* -ve: *Straightforwardness*

HIGH DOMINANCE

Strength: Straightforwardness

Note I have used the word "straightforwardness" here rather than the word "congruence" which is the element of trust described in chapter 2. *Straightforwardness* is the communication component of this element of trust. The other side of *congruence* is honesty, which has nothing to do with behavioral style. People who are high in Dominance typically do not hesitate to let you know what they think. They say what they mean and mean what they say. In fact, sometimes you wish they weren't so eager to tell you, or would at least do it with more empathy! They are *straight-shooters* and pride themselves on their ability to *call a spade a spade.*

Limitation: Acceptance

You've heard the expression: *They don't suffer fools gladly.* This often epitomizes the feeling people high in the D dimension have towards many people, particularly those who do not communicate directly or appear to be indecisive or slow. They can be *impatient* and *intolerant* of people because of their high *sense of urgency* and need to *achieve results.* More than anyone, this style needs to work on valuing differences in others, and to recognize and appreciate the strengths that other styles bring to the situation.

The two "D" team members in the example above did not hesitate to be *straightforward* about what was on their cards, and one was very quick to judge Simon as untrustworthy and attempt to take the bucket away from him.

HIGH INFLUENCE

Strength: Openness

People high in *Influence* love to talk and are the most emotionally open people in the **DiSC® Model**. They will tell you how they feel, and they want to know what's on your mind. They have a tendency wear their hearts on their sleeves, and therefore are more *self-revealing*; sometimes too *self-revealing*—they may tell you some very personal things about themselves that you didn't really want to know!

Limitation: Reliability

People high in *Influence* are the ones most likely to have a reputation for always being late. They're just so busy! Because of their strengths of *enthusiasm, optimism,* and *energy*, people with this style frequently *over-commit* themselves and then have trouble following through on all of their commitments. As mentioned above, *self-discipline* is the key for the *Influence* dimension. It does not come naturally, so it must become conscious. Stop and think. Pause. Count to ten (well, maybe five) before committing yourself.

Notice in the example of the executive team above, that it was the team member who was high in *Influence* who blurted out what was on his card as soon as he opened it. He did not stop and think about the fact that the envelope had said "private and confidential". He was operating instinctively, which for this style means: *Let's get it out in the open and talk about it!* In this situation, it was an appropriate response. However, there are times when his tendency to blurt things out without thinking would be inappropriate and diminish the trust others have for him.

HIGH STEADINESS

Strength: Acceptance

Accepting others is very important to people who are high in the "S" dimension because of their own need to be *accepted by others*. Their focus is on *giving support* to others. They get personal satisfaction out of doing things for others, and do not expect anything in return. They take others' needs into account when they are making decisions because the last thing they want to do is offend anyone or hurt their feelings.

Limitation: Straightforwardness

Because of their fear of hurting others' feelings, people who are high in *Steadiness* feel uncomfortable being direct with people, especially with bad news. Their natural tendency is to be *hesitant* in communication, preferring to think things through before saying anything to make sure they won't get a negative reaction.

Others may perceive this thoughtful silence as an indication that they are not listening, or worse, being evasive. Just because there is no immediate response does not mean they are not listening—give them time to think it over and respond. If you are high in the "S" dimension, you need to learn to communicate more directly, give straight answers, and be willing to risk offending people with the truth. To do this, you need believe in yourself and recognize that you contribute as much as anyone else. Only then will you be able to be *straightforward* with people about how you really think and feel.

The executive team member who was high in the "S" dimension in the example above did not play a very big role in the story. He did not have any trouble being *straightforward* with other team members about what was on his card, because the others had already spoken up.

HIGH CONSCIENTIOUSNESS
Strength: Reliability

People who are high in the *Conscientiousness* dimension are strong on *self-discipline*. If they say they'll do it, it's as good as done. Before making a commitment, they think through all the implications to make sure they can *follow through*. When they agree to do something, you can be sure it will be done accurately, and to a high standard of quality. If information is confidential, you can rely on this style to keep it confidential.

Limitation: Openness

There are two primary reasons People high on *Conscientiousness* may lack *openness*. First, they do not want to divulge information until they are certain it is correct. Second, they have a high need for *privacy*. They are cautious about trusting people, so they tend not to volunteer much information about themselves until they get to know you. If you are high on the "C" dimension, you need to understand that others have a need for more information. Think about what others might like to know, and volunteer it rather than waiting to be asked.

The team member high in the "C" dimension in the example above, Simon, refused to divulge to the rest of the team what was on his card, because it had said "private and confidential" on the envelope. As far as he was concerned, anything that is private and confidential, you keep to yourself. He did not stop to think about the impact his decision would have on the *trust level* in the team, because his focus was on *sticking to the rules*. Simon was primarily responsible for the breakdown of trust in his team. Had he stopped to think about his options—to reveal or not to reveal what was on his card—and what the consequences of each would be on the ability of the team to work together effectively, the answer would have been obvious.

Building Trust with People Who Are Different

This is one of the most important ideas in this book: each behavioral style judges others' trustworthiness by their own strength in building trust.

- People high in Dominance trust people who are straightforward
- People high in Influence trust people who are open
- People high in Steadiness trust people who are accepting
- People high in Conscientiousness trust people who are reliable

While it is important to be conscious of using all four **Elements of Trust**™, special emphasis must be placed on meeting the expectations of the person whose trust you want to gain. The biggest challenge for all of us is when we need to build trust with someone whose style is the opposite of our own.

The implications of this are enormous!

If you are high in Dominance and you have someone who is high in Steadiness in your team, it would be easy for trust to break down between you, even though you are both *trustworthy*, simply because of your differences in behavioral style. The same thing can easily happen between the *Influence* and *Conscientiousness* dimensions. Building trust requires conscious and persistent effort. If you are not working at building trust with your team members all the time—thinking about the impact of your behavior and decisions on the trust level—you may well be diminishing trust without realizing it.

It takes conscious effort for:

- A person high in *Dominance* to be accepting and attentive to someone high in *Steadiness*.
- A person high in *Steadiness* to be direct and brief with someone high in *Dominance*.
- A person high in *Conscientiousness* to share thoughts and feelings with someone high in *Influence*.
- A person high in *Influence* to produce the quality and detailed work expected by someone high in *Conscientiousness*.

The reward for putting in the effort and focusing on using these behaviors to build stronger trust relationships is the opportunity to build a *high-performance team*. How successful you are will be determined by your willingness and ability to adapt your behavior.

Using DiSC® as a Leader

As you can see, creating a work environment which meets the needs of all styles can be quite a challenge. The important thing here is *awareness*. If you are *aware* of each of your team member's needs, then you can work towards creating balance. The outstanding needs of each style are distinctly different and give you important insights into what drives each individual's passion. Human beings are more complex than having just one outstanding need. Most people are strong in two of the four dimensions of **DiSC˚**; therefore, most of your team members will have two of these needs that are important to them. Having each of them take a **DiSC˚** profile would really help you zero in on each team member's needs and how to get the best out of each person.

We have covered many factors in this chapter, and we will address many more in later chapters that can help you *light the fire within* your team members. But before we go on to the next chapter, I would like to focus on one of the biggest obstacles you face to effectively applying behavioral adaptability: *You cannot build passion in people you are irritated with!*

There are many things people do instinctively on a daily basis because of their **DiSC˚** behavioral style that are irritating to people who are different from them. They do not mean to irritate; in fact, they do not even realize they are being irritating. What this means is that you also irritate other people just by being yourself!

I have heard people say, *"Why shouldn't I get irritated when someone does something stupid? They deserve it!"* Well I can think of two reasons. First, it will not help you achieve your dream; you cannot expect people you get irritated with to be passionate about what you want them to do. Second, when you let someone irritate you, you give that person control over you—you are letting his or her attitude or behavior dictate your reactions.

When you do get irritated with someone, what do you do? Do you act out your irritation? When someone's natural behavior irritates you, you believe, in effect, that the person should not be that way. That is, you are judging *who they are* as wrong, bad, or inappropriate. You are doing the opposite of *acceptance, judgment*. And when you *judge* people rather than *accept* them, trust is diminished, and along with it their passion and commitment to you as their leader.

I am not suggesting that you should accept inappropriate behavior or poor performance. I am talking about how you feel about the people around you and how you behave toward them. Being aware of what irritates you and why it irritates you is very important. To get the best results out of this chapter, make a list of the things your team members or other people in your organization do that irritate you. Then respond to these questions for each item:

1. To what extent is what irritates you a difference in behavioral style?
2. Why does it irritate you? What are your beliefs about this behavior that cause you to get irritated?
3. What belief or alternative way of viewing this behavior would make it less irritating?

Doing this will help you learn to manage your emotions and your behavior more effectively, and create an environment where your team members feel more *accepted* and are able to *check their egos at the door.*

CHAPTER

Values – The Missing Link

One of my clients, a packaging company in Australia, employed about 100 people including a production-line worker named Alice. The company's focus was providing specialized packaging for other businesses. One example of what they did was package the knife, fork, and napkin passengers received on one of Australia's major airlines at that time.

Alice worked on a line packaging a collector's item for children, called a Tazo, to be inserted into packets of potato chips. Alice's company did not print or manufacture the Tazos, which were round disks; they just packaged and sealed them in cellophane wrapping to provide hygienic protection for the potato chips. One day, Alice noticed a particular batch of Tazos had blurred printing and, thinking that her children would not be happy to get a blurred Tazo, she reported this to her supervisor. The supervisor said, "It's OK, don't worry about it; let's run it anyway."

This response concerned Alice, so on her next break she reported it to the Quality Manager. He also said, "It's OK, don't worry about it!" Still not satisfied, Alice went straight to the CEO to express her concerns. The CEO called the Quality Manager in to his office to explain why they were packaging the defective Tazos, and he explained that the client knew they were defective, but they did not have any replacements and did not want to slow down their potato chip production schedule. The CEO thanked Alice for her courage in coming to him and for her concern for the quality of their products, and encouraged her to continue to speak up whenever she had concerns. It was more than lip service.

After Alice left, the CEO explained to the Quality Manager that it would have been more helpful if he had been open with Alice about the client's instructions to go ahead with the defective Tazos.

Why was Alice so concerned about the quality of the Tazos?

To understand that, let's go back a year earlier when the executive team made a decision that they needed to get all employees more committed to the organization's mission and vision. Part of the process I used in working with the executive team was to help them develop an initial draft of the core values they wanted everyone in the organization to operate by. I say *initial* draft because, to ensure that all employees are committed to the organization's core values, it is important for all of the employees to discuss, deliberate, and sign off on those values before they became final.

Among those values was one related to quality: "To exceed our customers' expectations with the quality of the products we produce."

Over the ensuing months, all managers, supervisors, and employees met to discuss the core values to determine whether they felt they were the right values. Could they all be passionate about operating by them? One group of employees challenged the quality value, explaining that customers expect the product to be perfect every time, so how can we exceed their expectations? When the employees were asked if they had any suggestions for a value statement about quality that they could be passionate about, one of the frontline workers called out, "We care about the quality of the products we produce!"

There was stunned silence for just a few seconds, then a chorus around the room of "Yes! That's it!" The organization's quality value statement was changed to the one employees were truly passionate about fulfilling.

Alice had participated in the discussions on the core values, and she really did care about the quality of what came off the production line. Even though the Tazos were not made by her company (they were just packaging them), she felt strongly enough about their lack of quality that she was prepared to go all the way to the CEO because the quality did not reflect the values everyone in the organization had agreed to. So, while some supervisors may see Alice as a troublemaker, she operated completely within the core values of the company. Here was a *switched on, passionate* employee who, because her organization had made a commitment to their core values, had not only the trust of her managers (most of them, anyway) to voice her disapproval, but also the empowerment to speak up and make it better.

Don't you want your team members to be like Alice: as passionate as you are about the quality of what they produce?

There are two sets of values that are the key to achieving this level of passion:

- **The Core Values** of the organization, which everyone in the organization <u>must</u> believe in if the organization is to achieve what it is capable of.
- **The Personal Values** of the individuals in the organization <u>must</u> align with the organization's core values.

Why Core Values?

Values drive *behavior*. If you think back to the **Whole Person Concept,** values have a strong influence on feeling and thinking, and therefore on behavior. In an organization that does not have an agreed upon set of values, people have no choice but to operate by their own values. This, of course, means that people may be operating by very different sets of values, resulting in inconsistencies at best, and conflict at worst. Establishing a set of *core organizational values*, if done correctly, makes it very clear what standards of behavior are expected of everyone in the organization. Put simply, it states <u>how</u> the organization operates in relation to everyone you deal with: employees, customers, suppliers, and the community.

Some mistakes organizations make in articulating their *core values* are:

- **Too many values**. People have difficulty remembering more than five or six items in a list. If employees cannot remember what your values are, if they have to look them up in the company handbook every time, you can be sure they will not be operating by them all the time. My recommendation is a maximum of six *core values*, but if you can reduce them to four or five, that is even better.
- **Too few or too many words.** Some organizations just have single words for their values with no explanation for what that value means. For example: *Integrity*. You might think that everyone knows what "integrity" means but ask ten people and you'll usually get ten different interpretations. Use too many words, and again, people will have trouble remembering.
- **Using platitudes**. For example: "*Our people are our most important asset.*" Almost every organization says that, but very few actually operate as if it is true. It's important to be as original as you can and say something that is meaningful for your organization.
- **It's not memorable.** People cannot operate by value statements that they cannot remember. Platitudes aren't memorable—and if they are, they're remembered with cynicism. Bland, matter-of-fact statements that don't inspire people are also not memorable.
- **Confusing values with goals or strategies, particularly financial goals.** About ten years ago, one of the major rental car companies in Australia was fined $1 million for price-fixing, which, of course, is illegal. One of their

Regional Managers colluded with the Regional Managers of other rental car companies in the same geographic area to fix prices above the going rate in order to increase his profit margin and, as a result, earn a higher bonus. In his defense, the Regional Manager argued that he was operating by his company's values because *profit* was in fact one of the company's values.

Profit is a goal, not a value. Yes, it is essential, but it is the natural outcome of running a successful business, not a value or behavioral standard that describes how everyone in the organization is expected to operate.

This Regional Manager neglected to mention that *integrity* was also one of the company's values. Not only did the company have to pay the fine, which exceeded their profits in the region for that year, but the company's image was damaged for a number of years to come. The problem occurred because both *profit* and *integrity* were listed as values, which created conflict in the regional manager's mind as to which was more important. Since most of the communication from head office down seemed to place more importance on *profit*, it made sense to him that *profit* was the more important value.

Values and Profit

For their best-selling book ***Built to Last***, authors Jim Collins and Jerry Porras researched eighteen companies that had been in business for fifty years or more that had positively impacted society and were widely admired and respected. They compared these visionary organizations with similar companies in the same industries that had not achieved the same level of success.

Their research shattered a number of myths that the non-visionary companies operated by. One of the foremost myths was: *The most successful companies exist first and foremost to maximize profits.*

The reality is: "…'maximizing shareholder wealth' or 'profit maximization' has not been the dominant driving force or primary objective through the history of visionary companies….Yet, paradoxically, the visionary companies make more money than the more purely profit-driven comparison companies."[10]

In the book ***Hidden Value***, Jeffrey Pfeffer and Charles O'Reilly III document research on eight organizations that achieved extraordinary performances out of ordinary people. Companies such as Southwest Airlines, SAS Institute (a software company based in Cary, North Carolina), Nucor Steel (also featured in Jim Collin's book ***Good to Great*** as one of the "good to great" companies), AES Power Corporation, and Cisco Systems. What Pfeffer and O'Reilly found is that these eight organizations achieved exceptional results by putting *values* and culture first—even before *profit* and stock price.[11]

These two books are just a small part of the research which has established that organizations that put values ahead of profit are more profitable than their competitors who are primarily focused on profit. Yes, there are examples of successful organizations that are primarily focused on making profit. My question is: *Would they be more successful if they put values first, and got all employees passionate about giving their best?*

I don't want to put too much emphasis on the financial reasons for putting *values* first. When you put *values* first because it is the right thing to do, the financial results will follow. What are your own *personal values*? Will you compromise your own *personal values* for financial reward? How is that different from prostitution? Answer: it really isn't. So if you wouldn't do it personally, why is it OK for your company to put *profit* ahead of *values*?

Do Your Personal Values Belong at Work?

Many leaders will say, *"It's not personal, it's business."* In other words, *"Don't take this personally, but I have to do the wrong thing by you to make more profit for my business."* When people presume they can separate their business values from their personal values—that they can have two sets of values operating simultaneously—they delude themselves. Either you believe something or you don't! If you compromise your personal values for business reasons, then your behavior is a truer reflection of your real personal values.

Personal values are values that are important to you in all aspects of your life. It is the way you believe you ought to live your life. It is what you believe to be right or wrong. There are many factors that have influenced your *personal values*: your race, your family upbringing (including religion and politics), where you grew up geographically (not just country or town but which part of town), and your life experiences. In the **Whole Person Concept**, we discussed that values and beliefs are learned. The fact that you believe them to be true does not mean that others will, or even should, share your beliefs.

Can we agree on *personal values* in the workplace? Yes…and no. There are some *personal values* that we do not need to agree on to work together effectively. For example, beliefs about religion or politics need not impact how we work together. We must be willing to accept that other people's values in these areas are right for them and my values are right for me. And yes, there are *personal values* that we can share in the workplace. If you believe that having passionate people with a high level of trust is essential to achieving your dream, it would make sense to ensure that everyone in your organization or team operates by the **Values That Build Trust™**.

Values That Build Trust™

Integro's research identified two values behind each of the **Elements of Trust**™. This means if you don't believe in the value itself, then you won't use the trust-building behavior that accompanies it. Further research over the past two years of over 5,000 employees in over forty companies in three countries found that these eight values are important to virtually everyone. When asked how important each value was on a scale of one to ten, almost everyone scored a 9 or 10 on all eight values. Let's look at these eight values and how they relate to the **Elements of Trust**™.

The Values That Build Trust ®

Copyright 2006 Integro Leadership Institute

VALUES THAT BUILD CONGRUENCE: Straightforwardness and Honesty

In an organization where expectations are not clear, there is a lack of *straightforwardness* about what is expected. Employees need to know what is expected of them. The Gallup Organization research shows that less than 50 percent of employees are clear about what is expected of them at work each day. That's because people will not be *straightforward* with each other. If we asked managers how clear they were about what employees expected of them, the percentage would be even worse. You cannot build a high *level of trust* without a high level of *straightforwardness* from you to your employees, and vice versa.

108

Honesty is a given; everyone would agree we need honesty in the workplace. So, why is it that so many research studies show that employees do not rate the *honesty* of their leaders as high? How much dishonesty is there in your workplace? What is an *honest* day's work? How would your employees respond to this question? If this has not been agreed on, employees will make up their own rules. What is *honesty* in terms of your products and services? How would your customers answer this question? What is *honesty* in compensation? Do all employees in your organization get *honest* value for what they contribute to the organization?

Any lack of *honesty* in these crucial areas is costing your organization. When employees perceive a lack of honesty, *rebellious* behavior increases. It is not difficult to foresee this happening.

What are your personal standards of *honesty*? Have you defined what you will and will not do as a leader?

VALUES THAT BUILD OPENNESS: Receptivity and Disclosure

One of my clients in Australia was a cotton ginning company. During the time I was working with them, we established a number of cross-functional task teams to identify areas where organizational performance could be improved. One of the ginning managers had been thinking for some time that there must be something better to do with the waste from the cotton pods than to have it sent off to a contractor each season to burn. The cost of having the contractor take the waste away from each gin added up to a total of $600,000 a year! This manager thought that since the waste from the cotton pods was natural and fibrous, there must be something else it could be used for, rather than just paying for it to be taken away to burn. He presented this idea to his task team, and after some research was done, the team found a company that was willing to purchase half the waste within the first year to make fertilizer; the next year, the company took the entire waste from the organization. So a $600,000 cost was turned into a revenue stream as a result of giving this manager an opportunity to *disclose* his idea. Within two years, this one idea resulted in close to a million dollar improvement per year on the bottom line.

How many valuable ideas lurk in the minds of your team members waiting to be disclosed?

The value of *receptivity* must come first. Without it, people will not be willing to speak up and *disclose* their ideas and opinions which, quite possibly, could save you money. There are many factors that influence *receptivity* in an organization. Who is more likely to be listened to: someone in senior management or someone on the frontline? If it is the case in your organization that the ideas of the people on the frontline are not valued as much as those of a senior manager, employees will know—and have probably already experienced it firsthand. When people are not listened to, they stop talking, and their ideas are never heard. They think, "*What's the use?*"

Many other factors may impact *receptivity* in your organization. Some people are more *receptive* to ideas from males than females, or vice versa. Your position in the organization, your length of time with the organization, and your academic qualifications, or lack thereof, can also have an impact on whether your ideas are listened to. Most of these scenarios are happening in every organization. Most people do not intentionally dismiss the ideas others have because of these factors—they just do it unconsciously. It is essential that you make people conscious of the importance of *receptivity*.

The best way to find out whether *receptivity* is high in your organization is to ask people, "*Do you feel comfortable expressing your opinions or sharing your ideas?*" The problem is if you ask this question and they are already not comfortable speaking up, they will not tell you and you will not learn the whole truth.

Until the value of *receptivity* is widely practiced, we cannot expect people to speak up or *disclose* their ideas and opinions, especially if their opinions are not popular. How are conflict and disagreement handled in your organization? Are people encouraged to disagree, or is disagreement something that is not tolerated?

Creativity and innovation are essential for your organization to achieve what it is capable of. To tap into the creativity of everyone in your organization, it is important that all employees speak up when they have an idea about how to improve things or when they see things that are not working. To truly value *disclosure* means encouraging your team members to share their opinions and insights whether they are popular or not. Obviously, these two values are very dependent on each other. You cannot have one without the other. People who are not listened to are not passionate!

VALUES THAT BUILD ACCEPTANCE: Respect and Recognition

I recently had the pleasure of meeting Peter Yarrow of Peter, Paul, and Mary fame. He was speaking and singing at a labor management conference in Los Angeles at which I was also a speaker. Peter told us about an organization he created called "Operation Respect," which has developed a program to teach children to respect each other. Peter, Paul, and Mary recorded a song called "Don't Laugh at Me" that is used in this program to help children find their common sensitivity to the painful effects of disrespect, intolerance, ridicule, and bullying. The program has been enormously successful and is now being taught in schools around the world. It occurred to me while listening to Peter that this is exactly what we at

Integro are working toward in organizations: *creating a workplace where everyone is respected and no one is treated with disrespect.* That is a workplace where anyone would want to work!

Behind *acceptance* are the values of *respect* and *recognition*. People need to be valued for who they are, not just for what they do. It is much easier to give people credit for what they have done, but it is more important to them to be valued for who they are. This is the first step toward *acceptance*. As we talked about in the last chapter, sometimes people will irritate you or make mistakes or not do things how you want them done, and you will need to get people to change what they do or change their behavior. **But that doesn't have anything to do with changing who they are as a person!**

Is there anyone in your organization you have difficulty *respecting*? What is it about this person you find difficult to *accept*? Is there anything about this person that you do admire? Does he or she have talents that are valuable to the organization?

When I have difficulty *accepting* someone, I find after reflection that it is usually a *values conflict*. The other person operates on different values and beliefs than I do. If I see someone belittling other people, for example, I have difficulty *respecting* that person because, according to my values, you never have an excuse to belittle anybody. You might have a reason to be critical, but not to belittle. If I happen to work with a person whose values conflict with mine, and I need to *build trust* and talk with him or her about what I perceive to be a *values conflict*. We will not be able to work together until I gain *respect* for that person.

Recognition is letting people know that you value what they do. Everyone understands the power of *recognition* and the part it plays in motivating people to give their best performance. Still, most employees think they do not get the *recognition* they deserve. They always want more. Why is it so hard for managers to give employees positive feedback? It doesn't cost anything, and yet it can have a significant impact on performance. A very positive impact!

There are mangers who believe they shouldn't have to give people *recognition*. While consulting for P & O Cruises in Australia some years ago, I met a human resources manager who was a good example of this. We did an employee survey to identify areas where the organization was doing well and find areas for improvement. One of the areas that scored most poorly was *giving employees recognition*. This upset the human resources manger. He fumed, "Employees are paid to do their jobs. Why do they need recognition as well?"

People <u>are</u> paid to do a job, so he had a point. When people apply for a job, they understand that in order to get paid, they need to do that job. It's very logical. But people have feelings, too. In the **Whole Person Concept**, people do not leave any part of themselves behind when they come to work. It is a fact that most people respond very positively to *recognition*. Why not give it to them when they need, want, or deserve it—especially if it contributes to them performing at their best?

Some organizations believe that the key to increasing motivation is to offer *recognition* in the form of financial incentives. But, as Jim Collins says in his monograph **Good to Great and the Social Sectors**[12], "The comparison companies in our research—those that failed to become great—placed greater emphasis on using incentives to 'motivate' otherwise unmotivated or undisciplined people."

To create a great organization, you must create an environment where people are self-motivated, self-disciplined, and will go to extreme lengths to give you their best every day. *Recognition* and *respect* will help you establish that environment. Look for opportunities to give positive feedback whenever your team members do something well, even if it is what they are paid to do. Demonstrate your respect for your team members by showing an interest in them, getting to know them, and asking for their input on how team performance could be improved. If they give you their best effort every day—which is your goal as a leader—they need to know you appreciate it.

VALUES THAT BUILD RELIABILITY:
Seeks Excellence and Keeps Commitments

Basically defined, *reliability* is: *I do what I say I'll do*. Some take it literally, giving only the minimum they need to stay out of trouble and committing no more that what it takes to keep their job. For that reason, one of the values behind the element of *reliability* must be *seeks excellence,* which Integro defines as: *"striving to do your best in everything you do."* In our research of over 5,000 employees, we asked them how important it is for them personally to operate by this value, on a scale of one to ten. **The average score was an astounding 9.6!** That means virtually all people want to give their best in everything they do.

Still, I've spoken with many managers who claim people don't want to—or won't—willingly stretch themselves; they believe their employees just want to do the minimum they can get away with and collect their pay at the end of the week. I suppose this belief is consistent with the kind of manager who thinks only money motivates people. And yes, there are employees who will tell you they don't want to do their best, because at this point in time, they are either *compliant* or *rebellious*. However they still respond in our research with a 9 or 10 out of 10 on *seeks excellence*, because deep down, they don't want to be bored, resentful, or rebellious—they want to use their talents and make a difference.

People get tremendous satisfaction from doing something well. Children enjoy most the activities they are best at, and adults are no different. Since we know virtually everyone wants to give his or her best, it makes sense for you as a leader to create that opportunity. We will talk more about that in later chapters as we look at identifying team members' talents and helping them develop those talents more fully in their work.

The second value behind *reliability* is more obvious: *keeps commitments*. You cannot rely on employees to do their jobs if they do not fulfill their responsibilities. Our research shows this value is extremely important to everyone; the average score for *keeps commitments* was also 9.6. Employees really want to do what's expected of them. Your job as their leader is to make sure they have the opportunity to do just that.

Organizational Values Are Not Enough

Remember Alice, the frontline worker in the packaging company? We've already established that she was committed to her organization's *core value* in relation to quality: "We care about the quality of the products we produce." Alice also knew that her CEO would support her in operating by those values because he made a commitment to all employees that they could come directly to him if they felt organizational values were being compromised. But would she have gone up to the CEO's office if her own *personal values* had not been in alignment with the *organization's values*?

We've looked at eight personal values that virtually everyone believes to be important. In Alice's case, the *personal values* that she demonstrated most clearly in her actions were *straightforwardness, honesty, disclosure, seeking excellence,* and *keeping commitments*. She knew her CEO believed in these values and that he'd be *receptive* and *respectful* of her for speaking up. If Alice did not believe in these *personal values*, then her passion to improve the quality of the products she produced would not have taken her from the factory floor to the CEO's door.

Could any employee be committed to and passionate about the value "We care about the quality of the products we produce" without a commitment to the eight **Values That Build Trust™**? Can you get employees committed to <u>any</u> of your organization's *core values* without the **Values That Build Trust™**? Most organizations have a *core value* related to customer satisfaction or costumer focus. If employees are going to really deliver on that value and delight your customers, they need to be *straightforward, honest, receptive, disclosing, respectful, seek excellence,* and *keep commitments*.

The same would apply if you looked at your organization's *core values* for innovation, integrity, or teamwork. One of the main reasons that most organizations struggle to get employees committed to operating by their *core values* is that they have not established or agreed to operate by *personal values* to which everyone in the organization is committed. It's not enough to expect just the employees to operate by these values; it requires an organization-wide commitment from the top down. When employees know that every leader in the organization believes in and operates by these values, the natural passion they have for striving to do their best, keeping commitments, and speaking up with ideas for improvement is unleashed.

As a leader, you can't begin your journey of taking your team from *engagement* to *passion* unless you are also committed to these *personal values*.

Why Values Are the Missing Link

In Chapter 3, we looked at the **Personal Responsibility Model** that described three kinds of people: *rebellious, compliant,* and *self-directed.* We also established that for your organization to achieve what it's capable of—and for you to achieve your dream—you need passionate people. The **Responsibility-Based Culture Model** highlighted the importance of *trust* and a leadership approach that *believes in people* and *partners* with them to create a great organization. In that model, we saw the risk behind the *authority-driven* model, which uses a *control-based* leadership approach designed to ensure compliance. This approach results in both *compliant* and *rebellious* behavior, and you cannot achieve your dream for your organization when people behave that way. This is one of the most challenging things for a leader to do: *to stop using authority-driven behavior, stop trying to control people, and start trusting them.*

One reason I hear managers say they cannot trust certain people in their organization is that the employee does not have the competence to do the job without supervision. If that is the case, what are you doing to develop their competence so they can do the work without supervision? If you can't trust employees to work without supervision, it's because you have not established a set of agreed upon values or properly trained your staff. Either that or you have people who are not trustworthy. If so, why did you hire them? If you know they aren't trustworthy, why are you keeping them?

Do you need to know where your significant other is every minute of the day? Do you need to know what he or she doing? If your answer is no, you obviously trust your partner. But if your answer is yes, then you really do have a trust problem. Assuming you do trust your partner, I suspect it is because you know that he or she will always operate, at least instinctively, by the **Values That Build Trust™**.

When everyone on your team has agreed to operate by the **Values That Build Trust**™ and your organization's *core values*, you no longer need to control people. You can trust them to do the right thing and to ask if they need clarification. You will know that all your employees are coming in to work every day committed to doing their best and fulfilling their responsibilities.

Pfeffer and O'Reilly's book, ***Hidden Value***, really reinforces this argument. As previously mentioned, the organizations that had achieved extraordinary performance from ordinary people put *"values and culture first... even before stock price!"* Other key factors in their success were: *"making the values real"* through *alignment and consistency.* They "hire for cultural fit," ensuring that the individual's values support the values of the organization, and "emphasize intrinsic rewards of fun, growth, teamwork, challenge, and accomplishment." [13]

Values really are the missing link when it comes to increasing engagement and passion. Get your team talking about these values and how they as a team can apply them to improve their performance.

FROM **ENGAGEMENT** TO **PASSION**

This last section of the book is focused on the leadership skills you need to meet the five levels of employee needs identified in the Passion Pyramid™.

The Passion Pyramid™

© Copyright 2006 Integro Leadership Institute

CHAPTER

What Do Employees Expect?

I was having a discussion with a group of managers in a leadership program a few years ago about the *psychological contract* that exists between an employee and their employer. When an employee accepts a job, there is an unwritten *psychological contract* based on a set of beliefs both parties have about what each is entitled to receive and required to give in the relationship. From an employee standpoint, the *psychological contract* is what is expected of them in return for providing their skills and talents. What's interesting about the *psychological contract* is that employees feel that a promise was made to meet their expectations even if those expectations were never discussed. In fact, openly discussing these expectations is the exception rather than the rule. It's not unusual for employees to become unhappy and leave an organization because their expectations were not met, even if they've never communicated them.

The CFO in this group I worked with was speaking passionately about this point. "Why do they do that?" he said.

He continued, "I had a person working in our accounts department, a really good accounts clerk. Out of the blue she just resigned. I was really happy with her work, and when she resigned, I said, 'Why are you leaving? What's wrong?' She then went on to say how she never felt that she was really appreciated, that nobody really valued what she did, and that because she never got any appreciation she just wasn't really happy here. So she had decided to look for another job." The CFO was shocked. His thinking was that if she was unhappy, why didn't she just speak up? He told her things would change if she decided to stay, even offered her a pay raise. She decided against it. It turned out she was a high in the *Steadi-*

119

ness dimension according to **DiSC** and had already accepted the other job. There was no way she would let her new employer down; besides, she had already left emotionally some time ago.

Back to the CFO's question: *"Why do they do that?"* There is no concrete answer, but the result is that they just do. When Inscape Publishing, Inc. researched employee expectations a few years ago, they came across a study of exit interviews showing that 76 percent of people who had left their organizations because their expectations had not been met had also not told anybody what those expectations were. Interesting, isn't it?

The accounts clerk above did what most employees do in that situation. Should she have spoken up? Sure, but she didn't. The research implies that most people will not tell you when their expectations are not met. So, as a leader, you have a choice to make: *Are you going to be proactive and find out what your employees' expectations are and whether or not they are being met? Or will you be reactive and just hope that they are?* This chapter focuses on the eleven most common expectations employees have when they come to work, and how you can use this knowledge to get people motivated not only to do the job they are hired to do, but to be the best that they can be.

Expectations

Whether spoken or unspoken, expectations have a powerful impact on how we think, feel, and behave and play a huge factor in our attitudes toward work. People who have clearly defined, well-communicated expectations derive much more satisfaction and will be far more successful in their work even if all those expectations cannot be met. **The opportunity to express one's expectations and discuss them is actually more important than having the expectation met.**

These are the eleven expectations identified by Inscape Publishing's research:

- **Compensation:** People do have high expectations that what they receive is fair in the context of what they do, how well the company is doing, and how others in the organization are paid. One sure way to kill employee commitment and passion is to restrict or reduce employee *compensation* and benefits while maintaining or increasing what executives receive.
- **Autonomy:** You probably already know which of your team members have high expectations for *autonomy*. They are the ones who really want to be *self-directed*. They want to have more of a say in decisions that affect them and want to be able to use their knowledge and experience to think of ways to do the job better. Basically, they want to have some choice in what they do and how they do it.

- **Work/Life Balance:** People who have high expectations in this area want a life outside of work. They want to have time with their families and friends or time to pursue their own personal interests. They don't want to be so involved with their work that their personal life suffers. That does not mean that they are not fully committed, engaged, or even passionate about their work. They can still give you their best every day and be a significant contributor to the organization. In fact, employees are more likely to be all of that if they have a life outside of work as well.

- **Career Growth:** People with high expectations for *career growth*, want their current role to help them make progress toward their career goals. What they do and how well they do it is very important to them. They seek opportunities to develop their skills, gain increased responsibility and provide leadership to others.

- **Diversity:** People who have high expectations for *diversity* are eager to learn and value working with people from different backgrounds who have had different experiences. They enjoy discussions with people who have different opinions and learning from others who have different perspectives. They encourage divergent thinking and enjoy the process of exploring new ways of doing things.

- **Environment:** How people feel about their work *environment* has more to do with the relationships they have with other people at work than it has to do with the physical environment. For people who have high expectations in this area, having friends at work whose company they enjoy is very important.

- **Expression:** People have a need to *express* themselves through their talent and their values. The stronger the expectation for *expression*, the more involved people want to be, and the more they want to use their talents and have input into how their work is done. They expect their work to be interesting so they can *express* themselves fully.

- **Recognition:** People believe that getting the *recognition* they deserve is important, and therefore expect to receive it.

- **Stability:** People who have a high expectation for *stability* want to feel secure in their jobs and have an environment that remains relatively unchanged. They expect that as long as they do a good job, they will be able to keep that job. They also expect that what they do day-to-day will not change significantly.

- **Structure:** People who have a high expectation for *structure* want clarity. They want to know what's expected of them, what they're required to do, and how to do it. That doesn't mean they want to be told what to do and how to do it. They also want to know what others expect of them and what results they are expected to achieve.

- **Teamwork:** People who have a high expectation for *teamwork* expect to work in collaboration with others <u>and</u> that they'll be able to make a contribution. They want to work with people who share their knowledge and skills, cooperate with each other, and are committed to the team's purpose and goals.

Identifying Your Employees' Expectations

As a leader, one of your challenges will be how you identify what your employees' expectations are. Which expectations are being met? Which are not? Since 2001, we've used Inscape Publishing's **Work Expectations Profile** with our clients, and it has played a significant part in helping leaders discover what each employee needs to be more passionate about his or her work. It measures each of the above expectations except for *compensation.* Since everyone has strong expectations about *compensation*, it is included in the interpretation section of the profile report as the eleventh expectation.

In my experience, most people score high on between four and six of the ten expectations measured in the profile. Within each of these broad categories of expectations, there are between five and eight more specific expectations. For example, under the expectation for *autonomy*, a specific clause is: *"You want to help decide your goals."* Another example from the expectation for *balance* is: *"You expect your supervisor and colleagues to understand that wanting balance between work and other aspects of life does not mean that you do not value your job."* It is these more specific expectations that truly resonate with people and help them to clarify their most important expectation. When employees understand their expectations at this level, it is also much clearer which expectations are being met and which are not.

The **Work Expectations Profile** goes beyond just measuring which expectations are important and whether they are met or not met; the profile actually helps employees identify what actions they can take to get those expectations met. In the interpretation section for each of the eleven expectations (including *compensation*) there are three sets of suggested action items:

1. **Communicate:** To whom do you need to communicate your expectations in order to get them met?
2. **Initiate:** What steps can you take to meet your own expectations?
3. **Adjust:** In the event that this expectation cannot be met, can you live without it? Do you need to reconsider how important this expectation is?

What Are Your Expectations?

I'm sure that as you were reading through the eleven expectations, you were connecting with some of them more strongly than others. Think about the potential impact of your expectations on how you lead your team. As a leader, you will most likely have a high expectation for *autonomy*—you expect to be in charge and like making decisions. Some of your team members may also have this expectation, but find that they cannot get it met because you want to make all the decisions. Being aware of your own expectations is very important to ensure that you do not satisfy your own needs at the expense of the people in your team.

One manager in a leadership program I facilitated a few years ago was surprised by his employee's feedback in a 360 degree Leadership Development Assessment. Two of his employees had made literal comments to the effect that: "He steals our ideas and takes credit for them." Later, when we discussed his **Work Expectations Profile** and the impact the manager's expectations can have on their leadership behavior, sure enough, this manager had scored very high in the expectation for *recognition*. Therefore, he had a strong focus on making sure he got the *recognition* for anything that his team did. Unfortunately, this desire blinded his ability to see the damaging effect it had on his team members. Another danger is that leaders who have low expectations for *recognition* assume that their team is like them and that they don't need *recognition*, either.

All of these expectations can impact a manager's behavior and the environment he or she creates for the team. You need to look at both your high and low expectations. Recently, the *work/life balance* expectation has increased in importance, so a manager with low expectations for *work/life balance* is most likely focused on advancing his or her career and expects to spend extra hours at work. This manager may not value someone with high expectation for *balance*, and may even view it as a lack of commitment to the organization.

Always look at your own expectations in addition to your **DiSC**° behavioral style to get an understanding of the environment you are creating for your team members. What can you do as a leader to create an environment where your whole team loves coming to work because their needs and expectations are being met, they are committed to you as their leader, and they are passionate about giving you their best? If you don't get that environment right, you're not going to be lighting that fire within people.

Using Your People Skills to Increase Engagement

Understanding your own and your team members' expectations can also help you to apply the **People Skills Model**. An employee's unmet expectation is a problem. The more important the expectation is, the bigger the problem is. If you have built enough trust with a team member to get him or her to share with you an expectation that is not being met, you are at least identifying the problem, and can discuss potential solutions. By working with your employee to facilitate changes that result in a resolution of the problem, you have not only solved the problem, you've also satisfied a need. Trust grows from this. It may not have taken a giant leap, but it will have taken a significant step forward.

Ask your team to identify a problem (unmet expectation) they have that they have not shared with you before. Work with them to resolve the problem and to facilitate a change that results in the expectation being satisfied. You know that different people have different needs and expectations. By understanding each team member's *expectations* and **DiSC®** behavioral style you can start applying all four *people skills* to building trust with each person. As you build trust and their needs become more satisfied, the level of engagement will continue to grow, as will their willingness to be more *self-directed*. Some will be excited about taking on more responsibility, while others will hang on kicking and screaming to stay *other-directed*. People will move at different paces. This is the first step in the process of ramping up the trust and engagement levels and starting to get people to be *self-directed*.

I recommend that all employees have the opportunity to take the **Work Expectations Profile** and meet with their immediate manager or supervisor to discuss their expectations. Then together they can develop a plan to get more of their expectations met. Here is an example of an employee who has become a much more valuable asset to her organization as a result of her manager working with her to meet her expectations:

For a couple of years, Kate worked at a government agency and held a job which required investigative field work, accuracy, the ability to relate to and work with people in adversarial situations, and summarizing in writing many different types of reports. The first three requirements she handled smoothly, but the wheels fell off when it came time to write the reports. Kate was very intelligent and possessed exceptional auditory recall of interviews and observations. She was also aware of her situation and recognized the need to change, and therefore accepted coaching readily. There were two work expectations that were really important to Kate that were not being met: *environment* and *work/life balance*. Her workspace was a cubicle within a "sardine can" of other cubicles, where she could hear her neighbor drop a paper clip. The same strength in auditory recall made it extremely distracting for Kate to work in her assigned space. Her manager explored ways to help her make time management work to her advantage, and they both became more proactive and aggressive in seeking out places within the agency where a quiet environment was possible. On occasion, Kate was allowed to work at home with a laptop in order to meet deadlines. She became more accountable for her time and was able to adhere more closely to a schedule for completion of assignments.

Kate now works in a position within the agency where her interviewing skills are the key piece to the job requirements, and her value to the organization has increased significantly. Also, her office has a door—a simple but important need to meet her expectations for her work environment and increase her effectiveness as an interviewer.

If it is not possible for you to have your whole team take the **Work Expectations Profile**, don't just hope your team members' expectations are being met. Start asking them questions about which of the expectations are important to them. It may be easier for them to talk if you discuss it at a team meeting. If you want to get honest, open answers from them about this, they need to be comfortable talking with you. You need to have established a reasonably high *level of trust* for people to be able to actually speak up with any kind of clarity about their expectations and to have the courage to say, "*I have an expectation for this and it is not being met.*"

In the next chapter, we will look at the communication skills needed to discuss performance problems with employees, and what you can do to get the best performance out of each team member.

CHAPTER

Getting the Best Out of Every Team Member

When you think about what a mentor is, you generally think of people who are older and wiser than you. You think of them as people with more experience than you have. I introduced David McNally in Chapter 1 of this book as a mentor to me. He believed in me, even when I did not completely believe in myself, and brought me along in his new company. Again, I am forever grateful.

I am sure you have had many people in your life who mentored you, believed in your abilities and talents, and wanted to help you develop them.

The dictionary defines "mentor" as someone who is a "teacher" or a "trusted counselor." As we discussed, people also enjoy doing things at which they excel. It is natural for people to want to be better and improve their performance. Mentors play an important role in helping people be their best, and sometimes they come from places you least expect. Have you ever been mentored by someone younger than you? What about being mentored by your children?

My son, Martin, is a golf professional who teaches at a golf school on the Gold Coast in Australia, home to some of Australia's most challenging courses. While catching up on the phone late last year, I mentioned in passing a problem I had with my swing. My son made a simple suggestion and urged me to try it out next time I was at the driving range. I did, and could not believe the improvements I made in just the first few shots. I was amazed at how much better and more effortlessly I hit the ball. Six months later, I am playing at my lowest handicap ever and continue to improve. Thanks, Marty.

Taking advice from my son the golf pro may seem obvious, but what if I had not been willing to take advice from one of my children? I would still be struggling. Because I listened, I am playing better and enjoying the game a whole lot more.

Many managers are not receptive to advice from younger people or from those lower than them in the organization. Perhaps they should be. Good advice comes from all around us.

The second time I took my family skiing, we began with lessons on the bunny slopes. That gives you an idea of how adept we all were. Our entire class struggled like I did to just stay on our feet. Every time I fell, I could just imagine how what I fell on was going to bruise. I was getting really frustrated because I could not get the skis to turn when another student, a boy much younger than I, saw me struggling and suggested I push forward harder with my knees to get my weight on the front of the skis. "Like this," he said, showing me. The toes of my skis weren't getting any traction because they didn't have enough weight on them. Because I listened and tried it, it made an immediate difference. I remained on my feet for the rest of the day (well, at least most of it).

What if I had ignored the boy's advice? What if I had dismissed it and said to myself, "What does he know?" Fortunately, I was receptive to being mentored by someone younger and inexperienced and, as a result, the day was more enjoyable.

Who have you mentored lately? How did you feel when you saw them growing as a person? It felt pretty good, didn't it? Did you learn anything while teaching? Were you reminded to do something that you had fallen out of the habit of doing yourself? One thing many managers fail to understand is that the mentor benefits at least as much from mentoring as the person they mentor. Teaching reaffirms how things should be done to both the mentor and the student.

The boy who gave me the skiing tip certainly experienced some pleasure from seeing me handle my turns better, but it also reminded him to push his knees forward and keep his weight on the front of his skis. We all fell less that day.

Who Should Be the Mentor?

Some organizations implement mentoring programs that exclude a person's immediate manager from being his or her mentor. This comes from some archaic idea that managers should not get too close to the people they manage because they will have a difficult time disciplining or firing them. I do not object to mentoring programs providing people with guidance from sources other than their immediate manger or supervisor. I do, however, see a big problem when managers or supervisors cannot mentor their own team members. Leaders need to ignite passion in their team members; mentoring is an integral part of that and cannot be done without hands-on guidance.

Think about who has made a difference in your life as a mentor. See if these descriptions fit that person(s).

- **Listening Adaptability**. A mentor tunes into your wavelength and your feelings, not just listens to the facts about what you are saying. With David McNally, he could sense that I had doubts about my ability to be a consultant. He knew I would never achieve my potential if I didn't overcome those doubts by doing what I was afraid of. Hence his advice: *Bite off more than I could chew, and then chew like hell!*

- **Giving and Receiving Feedback**. Mentors can and will give honest, constructive feedback in a way you are willing to accept and learn from. They are also receptive to feedback from you, welcoming the opportunity to improve their own performance. David listened to me express my feelings of doubt. Instead of saying outright that I was wrong, he acknowledged my concerns and encouraged me to overcome that fear.

- **Counseling**. Mentors ask questions to help you make your own decisions about what you can do improve your performance. When you ask them for advice, they are more likely to ask you questions to get you to discover your own answers (i.e. use the Socratic Method) than tell you what to do. My son, Martin, used questions to help me discover what was not working with my golf swing.

- **Coaching**. Mentors help you develop your talents and skills, guide you toward the learning experiences you need, and learn from the unexpected and unplanned. They help you to see there are no mistakes except for those you do not learn from. The boy on the ski slopes was a good coach; he showed me how to turn instead of merely telling me.

Of these four skills, listening is paramount because it impacts the remaining skills. When you focus on these skills, you will better understand how mentoring ignites passion in your team.

A *Mentoring Model*

Why Do We Need to Learn to Listen?

When I attended school, there were no classes on the subject of learning to listen. None of my four children was offered a listening elective, either, so it appears as though nothing has changed. There were many courses on communication and presentation skills and I took a Dale Carnegie course on public speaking and participated in debate, but very few classes were available on listening. It's really a shame.

In the course of a workday, how much time is spent listening to someone over the phone, in a meeting, or in a one-on-one conversation? How often does ineffective listening or miscommunication occur?

Several years ago, I asked one of our administrative team members, Jane, to type up a multi-page document for me. "No hurry," I told Jane. "Any time in the next two or three days would be fine." I knew she had a lot of work on her plate, so I did not want to pressure her. Ten days passed and I realized I had not seen the document, so I went to Jane and asked her what happened. "It's right here," she said. "I've been waiting for you to come and get it."

I bit my lip and took the document back to my office to think through what had gone wrong in the communication process. When I'm asked to do something, I assume that the person who asked expects me to deliver it when it's complete. Obviously, Jane did not share this opinion. Still, she did exactly what I asked her to do, which was type up the document. I did not explicitly say, "Bring it to me when you are done," but assumed it would happen. I had to recognize my part in the failure of that communication to achieve the desired outcome. I did go back to Jane and discuss with her how we could both improve our communication in future by ensuring each person understands what is expected.

I am sure something like this has happened to you where you thought your point was effectively communicated but the final product was not what you asked for. Some people simply don't listen. When I call people, I always say who I am: *"Hello. My name is Keith Ayers."* Then I describe the reason for the call. One thing that frustrates me no end is that even though I told them my name, within thirty seconds they ask for it again!

Listening is Good for Business

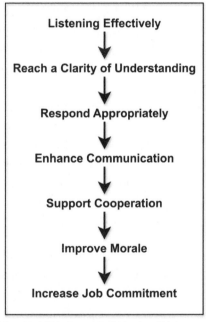

When you listen effectively, you understand more clearly what people are telling you. When you understand more clearly what people are telling you, you can respond more appropriately to what you have heard. As a result, your communication has been enhanced and improved. When communication is improved, you get increased support and cooperation. That leads to improved morale, engagement, and commitment to the job and to you as a leader. Increased commitment results in increased performance and productivity. **Effective listening makes good business sense.** It sounds pedantic to actually have to say that, but again, that is the irony: not enough people truly listen.

The Five Listening Approaches

I attended a business conference featuring a motivational speaker's presentation. As you would expect, he had a dynamic personality, just like most other "motivational speakers." After his presentation, I met two friends, Henry and Emily, in the lobby of the conference hall and talked about the presentation—which was, of course, designed to motivate us. We got to talking about the jokes and stories the speaker told as well as the overall message, which was where my two friends had fundamentally different perceptions. Henry appreciated the speech for what it was: entertainment. He enjoyed the jokes and anecdotes, which surprised Emily. She asked Henry, "You thought that was great? I didn't get anything out of it. I was looking for a message on how to improve sales and all I heard were stories and jokes."

The speaker's goal was to entertain us. So why did Henry love the presentation when Emily thought it was a complete waste of time? How did two people in the same profession, who both listened to the same speech, interpret it so differently?

Here is another example about mixed interpretations:

My wife and I met up with another couple to see a movie. Bob, the husband of my wife's friend, was in the movie-editing business. We agreed on a movie, got the popcorn, and went in to watch. Three of us—myself, my wife, and Bob's wife—enjoyed the movie. Bob did not. As far as the three of us were concerned, the movie was what it was: entertainment. For Bob, the movie was filled with technical flaws. Bob spared no breath illuminating the flaws until his wife, thankfully, told him to stop.

How could people form such differing opinions on the same information?

Research conducted by Inscape Publishing Inc. determined there are five distinctly different ways people naturally listen, called *listening approaches*. Your *listening approach* has an impact on how you communicate as well as how you listen.

- **Appreciative Listening**: Listening to appreciate what you're hearing to enjoy the experience and be entertained.
- **Empathic Listening**: Tuning into the feeling content of what the person is saying, showing that you care.
- **Comprehensive Listening**: Listening to understand the overall message, not necessarily the specific details.
- **Discerning Listening**: Listening to get all the facts and details and make sure you don't miss anything.
- **Evaluative Listening**: Listening in order to evaluate what is being said and make a decision.

Henry enjoyed the motivational speaker because he was an *appreciative listener*, in that he was prepared to accept the presentation as entertainment. Emily, on the other hand, listened *comprehensively* and *discerningly*, looking for factual information and an overall message, which she did not find.

Can you relate to this? Maybe you have experienced this in reverse, where the speaker gave lots of facts but delivered them in such a dry and boring way? This would have made Emily, a more *discerning* and *comprehensive listener*, happier and would have put Henry to sleep. Different strokes for different folks, I guess.

At the movies, my wife, Bob's wife, and I were comfortable with adopting an *appreciative listening approach* and just enjoying the movie. Bob, partly because of his training, but maybe also because of his natural *evaluative listening approach*, watched the movie with a critical eye to see if it matched up to his standards. It would be hard for Bob to enjoy any movie with his frame of mind, unless of course it measured up to his expectations technically.

Could Bob have adapted his *listening approach* and enjoyed the movie? With his technical background it may have been hard, but it was definitely possible. The opportunity to learn to put *evaluative listening* "on hold" comes later in this chapter. To be a successful mentor you must be able to do that. People say that good leaders wear many hats. **Good mentors wear different ears!**

APPRECIATIVE LISTENING

Appreciative listeners enjoy the experience for what it is, paying attention to more than just what is being said. For *appreciative listeners*, it's the whole play, not just the lines. They take in the ambiance and music, consider what they hear, have a pleasurable experience, and relax.

In the workplace, *appreciative listening* is best used when getting to know people. If a team member has a child who plays soccer and she tells you about it on a Friday, you ask about it on a Monday, "How was Joanie's soccer game last weekend? Did they win?" You can ask follow-up questions to display interest, but really you are just sitting back and listening. *Appreciative listening*, to some, may seem like a waste of time. But I can assure you that your team will not be passionate about working for you as a leader if it appears to them that you do not *appreciate* them.

EMPATHIC LISTENING

Let's say a team member, Karen, feels increased pressure due to more work caused by a corporate freeze on hiring. You notice her irritability and, at times, she seems flustered when making decisions. Asking her to work overtime to get the job done has put a strain on her as she cares for her young family.

Ask her about it and listen to her with *empathy*. Tune into her feelings and really allow her to talk. Maybe Karen is venting. Maybe there is not much you can do about it except show that you do care. Your focus through this listening approach is to be supportive, nod, and keep eye contact to show you really understand. Demonstrate this by reflecting back what you hear. For example: *"I'm sensing that you are really frustrated about that."* Show them that your time is never too important to listen.

Empathic listening may not involve providing solutions, but it goes a long way toward making you a leader who does not seem cold or aloof. People will not be passionate about working for a leader who doesn't care about how they feel.

COMPREHENSIVE LISTENING

Consider Jane and the document I wanted her to type. The only facts I communicated to her were to "type up the document and have it done in the next two or three days." Jane did exactly that, no more, no less. Had Jane listened *comprehensively*, she would have clarified what I wanted done with the document when she was finished. I take responsibility for the poor communication, since I was the initiator. *Comprehensive listening* requires two-way communication where both parties seek to clarify what the other is saying, and I could have made sure that happened.

With Karen, the employee feeling stressed about her increased workload, you used *empathic listening* to understand her need to balance her family and work priorities. Now you need to see whether you can decrease her stress by helping her be more efficient and effective. Ask her what she does on a day-to-day basis, what her challenges are, and how she thinks she can eliminate those challenges to be more efficient. Your questions help both of you understand the factors that can reduce Karen's work pressure. This conversation also allows Karen to think through the situation herself and arrive at her own solutions.

DISCERNING LISTENING

When you finish up a complex order over the phone with a sales representative, before hanging up you want to be absolutely certain that the representative understood your order completely. Being a *discerning listener* in this situation and double-checking the details ensures that when your order arrives, there will be no mistakes. At least, that is your hope.

Discerning listeners take in all the facts. It is the most thorough listening approach when it comes to detail. They take notes, repeat even the minutest detail back to be sure, and confirm what was communicated in the form of notes or other records. It requires a high level of concentration and can be time-consuming, but it has many useful applications in the workplace, especially now when so much information is available to us. Those who are not naturally strong in *discerning listening*, as I am, need to discipline themselves and put in extra effort into eliminating any distractions, taking detailed notes, and checking back to confirm that they have accurate information. This is one area where a lot of listening mistakes occur, because people just don't discipline themselves enough to pay attention to the details. Like the person who has to ask me again for my name!

EVALUATIVE LISTENING

Let's say you are shopping for a flat panel TV and go to a retail store to explore your options, still somewhat unsure of the pros and cons of plasma versus LCD or versus DLP, and so on. A salesperson approaches you and begins his pitch about the different kinds of TVs. How can you believe what the salesperson is telling you?

Making decisions on a purchase like this is a perfect time for an *evaluative listening approach*. You need to focus on your own needs so you can make the right decision based on the information provided. You need to question the information sender's motives. Is the salesperson recommending what is best for you, or the product they get the most commission on? *Evaluative listeners* express skepticism and challenge the speaker with questions that require evidence to back up claims. Ultimately, as an *evaluative listener*, you have the right to accept or reject the message, or just quit listening.

Evaluative listening is an important approach when making a purchase or deciding which political party you are going to vote for. But it can hinder your effectiveness when counseling and coaching members of your team. *Evaluative listeners* focus on their own agenda, so when someone approaches you with a concern like, *"I need some help with something. I am not confident on how to do this,"* you should not reply, as an *evaluative listener* might, *"Don't be stupid, you've got plenty of confidence, go for it."* You may tend to your immediate need, but you are essentially shutting down the conversation by demonstrating a lack of empathy and, perhaps, encouraging alienation from this team member. You will likely not get valuable input from people in the future if you use this listening approach inappropriately.

As a mentor, *empathic* and *comprehensive listening* are your primary tools, though *appreciative* and *discerning listening* have value in helping you build relationships and get the facts, respectively. Inscape Publishing, Inc.'s **Personal Listening Profile*** is a tool I use to measure a manager's *listening approach*. I've taken hundreds of managers through the profile but have seen very few score highly on *empathic listening*; not surprisingly, most managers score high on *evaluative listen-*

ing. If you are typical of most managers, then you have been trained well to listen *evaluatively*, to be judgmental in order to achieve results, and not to let emotions get in the way. Perhaps this is why so many managers find it easier to just tell people what to do.

If you are naturally strong in *evaluative listening*, it will be difficult to switch it off. While people are talking, you are going to be comparing what they are saying to what you believe. When you hear something you disagree with, some switch inside you will want to blurt, *"That's not true."* Thinking this is fine, but saying it could either shut down the communication or escalate the conversation into an argument. This does not help the mentoring process! Put your *evaluative listening* on hold and suspend judgment, at least for a while. You may need *evaluative listening* at the end of an interaction to help the person make a decision by giving some advice, but few other times is the *evaluative approach* the correct one when mentoring.

The best way to put evaluative listening on hold is to make sure that you repeat what you are hearing in your own words. For example: *"So what you're telling me is that you're feeling upset about what Bill said"* or *"If I understand you correctly, you believe we could get better results if we did it this way."* In the first example, you respond to the feeling content using empathic listening. In the second, the response is to something factual using comprehensive listening. To be able to focus on both factual and feeling content accurately, you must learn to put evaluative listening on hold and listen to what the other person is really saying—listen to understand, not to agree or disagree.

Practicing Listening Adaptability

To develop your *comprehensive* and *empathic listening* skills, interview someone on an emotion-laden topic. Grab a friend or colleague to practice with. You can say you are practicing this listening approach, but you don't have to. To the other person, it will simply be a normal conversation.

Start with a topic, for example: *"What is the major problem in the world today and how would you solve it?"* or *"What is the major problem you have in your organization today and how would you solve it?"*

Use topics that everyone, including you, has a strong opinion about. The stronger your views on a topic, the harder it is for you to hear someone else's opinion and stay out of *evaluative listening*. Since you already know what you think about the topic, your role is to interview someone else for at least eight to ten minutes without expressing your own opinion at all. To ensure that you stay in *comprehensive* and *empathic listening approaches*, make sure you do the following:

- Focus on the other person's feelings and ask questions to check the accuracy of your perception. For example: *"You seem to be very passionate about that?"*

- Focus on the factual content and ask that person to elaborate on points that you would like to know more about. For example: *"Tell me more about…"*

- Do not ask leading questions, give your own opinion, or agree or disagree with anything your partner says. Seek to understand the main message, main solution, and any supporting ideas. Ask questions to make sure you understand your partner's rationale behind his or her opinion.

- When you finish talking, summarize what you heard by saying: *"OK, so let me just check that I understood you correctly…"* Go on, in your own words, to repeat what your partner saw as the major problem and how he or she would fix it.

This exercise will be more challenging if the other person's choice of major problems or suggested solution is very different than what you believe the "problems" to be. You may want to test yourself and your ability to put *evaluative listening* on hold by doing this exercise with more than one person and choosing people with opinions different from your own, such as people who have a different political philosophy than you. This is exactly the kind of listening you need to be skillful at to be a mentor. Now, let's delve into the next mentoring skills. Good luck with the exercise!

Giving and Receiving Feedback

How you give feedback makes a huge difference in how it is received. It's the difference between helping and offending someone. Have you ever said anything that someone took offense to? What if that person's response was to attack you with something like: *"You are so insensitive! So pathetic! Don't you ever talk to me like that again or you'll regret it for the rest of your life."* Not a very comfortable feedback, right? How would you react? Defensively? What if the approach was more delicate? *"Bill, when you told me what you thought of my appearance today, I felt really hurt. I don't think you meant to hurt my feelings, but that's how I felt in reaction to what you said. I really would appreciate it if in future you could give more thought to how you communicate your feedback to me."*

When you hear the word "feedback," what do you think of? Typically, people think of feedback as bad news or a reprimand when they have done something wrong. Feedback has a negative connotation. Feedback can come out in a positive or negative way, but it is designed to improve someone.

Think about feedback as a gift. What do you do with gifts? You unwrap them, think about them, and accept the gift for what it is: a gift. Sometimes you don't need a gift, so you just put it aside. Sometimes you give it away to someone else. You can do that with feedback, too. Some feedback is difficult to accept. Your natural reaction may be to reject it because you know it is not true. But what if it is true?

During a personal development program I attended in Sydney, Australia about twenty years ago, one of the sessions featured information about different personality types. It wasn't a model that I had seen before or since, but it became clear as we worked through the various personality types that I best fit the perfectionist description. Although several of my descriptions fit the mold, I did not view myself this way and, in fact, really did not believe I was. Although some of the description of the perfectionist type did fit me, I did not agree that I was "picky" or "pedantic," so I dismissed the whole thing as not relevant.

A few days later, my daughter, Lauren, who was five or six years old at the time, came to me and showed me a drawing of a house she did at school that day. When coloring it in, Lauren, well, made it a little messy by going outside the lines. Before I knew it, I was pointing out a place where she went outside the lines and getting ready to say something like: "Darling, you went outside the lines here, and here..." I was literally shocked, thinking, "My God, I <u>am</u> picky and pedantic!" I removed my guilty finger from her drawing and thanked her for doing such a beautiful job for me. Now, if you had told me prior to that point that I would be picky or a perfectionist about my little daughter's drawings and tell her to color within the lines, then I would have said, "You've got to be kidding. That is not me."

To see that finger of mine pointing out the "imperfection" was a big learning experience. "Oh my God, I really do that. I point out, to my kids, when things aren't exactly right." That was such a huge gift for me to become aware that I was being pedantic with my children on things that, at their age, don't matter one little bit. If she wanted to color outside the lines, then why not let her? Today, Lauren is an exceptionally freethinking, creative, and adventurous spirit who definitely thinks outside the box.

Only when you look at feedback as a gift, unwrap it, open it, and think about it can you determine whether the feedback has any merit. Even if you ultimately know that the feedback is not accurate, isn't it worthwhile knowing what the other person was thinking about you? Do you want them to see you that way? If not, then what would you need to do differently in relation to them to change their perception? Giving and receiving feedback should be a positive experience for both parties. To achieve that, you have to learn to give feedback in a way that is effective and that people will accept.

THE GIVING FEEDBACK MODEL

I developed a simple model that helps me to give feedback, whether it is positive or negative, in a way that people are more likely to see it as a gift. As with any structured approach to communicating, it can seem a little artificial if you do it in too structured a way. The steps in the **Giving Feedback Model** are intended to be used as a guide.

The Giving Feedback Model has three steps:

1. **An Observation**: The description of the event, or events, that took place that led to the reason for you wanting to give feedback. Describe the event without any evaluation or judgment. In the earlier example, we said, *"Bill, when you told me what you thought of my appearance today...."* It's just a description of what happened.

2. **The Outcome**: What is the outcome of your observations? It could be how you felt or there may have been consequences as a result of an event. Then pause and wait for a reaction. In the example, the outcome was: *"I felt really hurt."* After pausing, it may lead to a discussion or you could simply pause to let it sink in, and then go on to Step 3.

3. **A Request**: Ask someone how you would like things to be in the future. The request was: *"I really would appreciate it if in future you would give more thought to how you communicate your feedback to me."* One of the reasons negative feedback usually does not work is because it is given in the form of a complaint.

People don't respond positively to complaints. They get defensive. Complaints are focused in the past, and we can't change the past. Requests focus in the future, which we can control to some extent. The request lets other people know how you prefer to be dealt with—respectfully—when the situation arises in the future.

Think of a situation where you gave someone feedback and that person reacted defensively. What did you say? And how did what you say fit with the **Giving Feedback Model**? Then, think about how you could restructure what you said using the **Giving Feedback Model**. Write that down or practice saying it and see whether you think that response might have produced a different outcome than your original response to that person's defensive behavior.

Now think of a situation where someone gave you feedback that you were not happy with, that you felt offended by, or that seemed inappropriate. Using the **Giving Feedback Model**, think of how that person could have restructured the feedback and how you would have felt if he or she had done that compared to how you actually felt.

So how is Bill going to respond in the example we have been using? Let's have a look at the **Receiving Feedback Model** so we can see how to respond to it.

THE RECEIVING FEEDBACK MODEL

The **Receiving Feedback Model** uses the same three components as the **Giving Feedback Model**, except the first two steps are in reverse order.

1. **The Outcome**: It is best to start your response to feedback by saying something like, *"if I understand you correctly…"* and then describe in your own words the *outcome*. In the more tactful version of the feedback above. Bill says, *"If I understand you correctly, you felt really hurt…"*

2. **An Observation**: Again, in own words, describe the event, as described to you, without any evaluation or judgment. Back to the example where Bill continues *"…when I was critical of your appearance today…"*

3. **A Request**: And again, in your own words, the request the other person made of you: *"…and you would like me to be more thoughtful in how I give you feedback in future. Is that correct?"*

Both parties can now go on to discuss the issue and come to an agreement on what they will do in future.

The purpose of the **Receiving Feedback Model** is to help you stay out of *evaluative listening* until you are sure that you have really heard the feedback and understood it correctly.

Now, use the **Receiving Feedback Model** to consider how you could react to feedback someone gave you that you were not happy with. Respond as if you had received the feedback in a positive way and you were responding to clarify and get confirmation on what the feedback really was.

The last two essential skills a mentor needs are *counseling* and *coaching*. While we are using these skills, we will be continuing to use the different *listening approaches* as well as the **Giving and Receiving Feedback Models** where appropriate.

Giving Feedback Model

> **"I want to talk with you about..."**
> *(Observation)*
>
> **"I noticed that..." (or, "I felt that...", etc.)**
> **Pause... allow for a response**
> *(Outcome)*
>
> **"What I would really like is..."**
> *(Request)*

Receiving Feedback Model

> **If I understand you correctly...**
>
> **"You saw..." (or, "You felt...", etc.)**
> *(Outcome)*
>
> **"As a result of..."**
> *(Observation)*
>
> **"and what you would like is..."**
> *(Request)*

Counseling

Eric, a customer service representative, arrives late for work once or twice a week. He is usually only ten or fifteen minutes late, but occasionally it is a half-hour. Eric is young, single, has a healthy social life, and tends to be a little disorganized. However, he has great communication skills, the customers really like him, and he is a valuable team member to you. As his supervisor, you've heard the grumblings from other employees about how Eric gets special treatment, so you decide it is time to deal with Eric's lateness once and for all, especially because it is affecting the other employees' interpretation of your leadership. You have spoken with Eric about it before, and he is always apologetic, but it is obvious that he does not really see it as a big deal because it continues to happen. When Eric is late, it automatically means his phone is not being answered and his calls are routed to other members of the team. So other people are doing Eric's work when he is not there. This could also result in customer complaints, or even lost customers, and other staff members are becoming resentful about the fact that Eric continues to come in late.

The purpose of *counseling* is to help the other person understand the current situation and that there is a need to do something different. It is important to address this need and get agreement from that person to make the change. Typically, we will use *counseling* when people are not ready or willing to be coached, don't realize there is a need to do anything differently, or don't believe they should have to change. Eric's example is a classic case where *counseling* is needed. He knows his lateness should change, but he hasn't been willing to make the change and he doesn't see it as being the problem that it really is. Helping Eric understand and getting his commitment to making that change allows you to follow through with coaching him to be on time.

When *counseling*, ask questions to help the other person explore his or her feelings, beliefs, and attitudes. Have the other person clarify his or her own thinking without expressing your own opinion or agreeing or disagreeing initially. You'll use mostly *empathic* and *comprehensive listening* to focus on the feeling and factual content of what that person is telling you.

Counseling is usually the most difficult part of being a mentor. It requires you to deal with people unwilling, or lacking the awareness, to change. You must challenge their beliefs and attitudes in order to get them to change. The good news is that you will be doing it by asking questions, so they will be doing most of the talking. Just listen.

Remember that you are doing the *counseling* to benefit the other person. Yes, the organization will benefit, too, but you are also helping the person you are *counseling* to grow. You may have already found that there are a lot of people who have low expectations of themselves. They don't see themselves as capable of achieving more or they have a limited view of their potential. Oftentimes, you will see more potential in people than they'll see in themselves. If you just accept their view, then they do not see a problem because they are staying where they are. Allowing this to happen ensures that they, you, and your organization will lose out on the opportunity to develop them to become the best they can be.

The first step to getting an agreement to change is to establish a clear understanding that there is a difference between the current situation and what is possible, expected, or desired. Give specific examples and be clear about your expectations. This is a good situation for using the **Giving Feedback Model** as a lead-in to the *counseling* discussion.

For instance: *"Jim, I'd like to talk to you about what looks to me like a hesitance on your part to step up into a leadership role. Like when I asked you if you'd like to take the lead role on the XYZ Project, you were very quick to decline* (An Observation). *I believe you have a lot more talent than you are able to use in your present role and I thought that this would be a great opportunity for you to develop your leadership skills* (The Outcome). *I really would like you to reconsider my offer. What do you think?* (A Request)"

The response to that situation will vary from person to person. Let's say Jim decides he really is not sure he wants to be a project team leader and comes back to you with, *"While I really appreciate your making this offer, I'm not really sure that I have the talent. I don't feel very confident about taking on this role. I'm also concerned that not doing it might adversely affect my future prospects with the company."*

To this response, some *counseling* questions you might ask are:

- Jim, what are your future plans for your career? Where do you want to be five years from now?
- What do you see as your primary strengths that enable you to contribute most positively to the team at this point in time?
- What if I'm right? What if you do have the talent to be a leader and you never tap into that opportunity? How would you feel a few years down the road when you're still thinking, "I wonder what would have happened, if I had taken that opportunity?"
- What impact would that have on your career?

If, in the long run, none of these questions actually work and Jim says, *"Look, I'm just not interested"* or *"I don't want to do that,"* then there is no point in pushing or pursuing it, other than to give him some time to think it over and continue to provide positive feedback. Continue to reinforce Jim with positive feedback, let him know that you believe in him, and give him time to reconsider. Some people take more time than others to build their confidence and make a decision that involves the kind of risk-taking that is associated with taking on a leadership role. In each case, a good mentor knows how to counsel each person individually to determine how ready and willing, as well as how capable, he or she is. Being an effective listener is an important tool for mentors to achieve this goal.

Understanding Consequences

When people don't realize there is a problem or don't see the need for change, they are usually not aware of the consequences of what they are doing. Using a questioning approach allows you to help other people discover the consequences for themselves, rather than tell them what they are. When they become aware for themselves, they can make the appropriate decision and take responsibility for it. In other words, they can be *self-directed*. When you tell them what to do, you encourage them to be *other-directed* and avoid taking responsibility for their actions.

There are two kinds of consequences: *automatic consequences* (things that happen automatically as a result of an action that is taken) and *imposed consequences* (they are imposed by someone in authority).

In our example of Eric arriving late for work, the *automatic consequences* were that his calls were answered by other team members, or not at all. One of Eric's customers could *impose* a consequence of moving to a competitor as a result of his poor service. His manager could also *impose* a consequence of disciplinary action or termination if he persists in being late for work. It is much better to gain a commitment to a change in behavior by focusing on *automatic consequences* that occur. *Imposed consequences* should be used only as a last resort. If you discuss *imposed consequences*, it is important that you can follow through and deliver the consequence. You lose credibility when you say you will impose consequences that you subsequently can or will not act on.

There are also positive consequences. When Eric is at work on time, his customers get their calls answered promptly, and they are more likely to be satisfied and loyal. His coworkers will also be more satisfied as they will not have to carry the extra workload.

Coaching

Coaching helps team members to set attainable goals, make effective decisions, cultivate detailed action plans, and get their continued commitment to follow through on achieving positive results. It is an important part of their development. Again, you want to ask questions rather than telling or giving advice. Your questions help your team members think through what they can achieve, what their goals are, and what knowledge and skills they need to achieve them. Then ask questions to get them to explore the options available and likely outcomes for each option.

Let's return to Jim, the team member hesitant to take on the leadership of the project team. Here are some questions you could ask him:

- If you were taking responsibility for this project, what would you see as being the most important priorities for you as the project leader?
- Think about leaders you have worked for on projects in the past. What are the things they did that really worked well for you?
- Are there any leaders you've worked for where you would say there were things that they did that didn't work for you or that you would not want to do?

The purpose of asking these questions is to draw on their experience of working for different leaders to say, *"What have you seen that works and what have you experienced that doesn't work?"* You get them thinking about what they need to do without actually having to tell them what to do.

Once Jim has described his perception of the leadership role, the next step is to identify what knowledge, skills, or experience he needs to be able to function in that role. You could ask these as separate questions:

- What additional knowledge do you feel you need to be competent in that role?
- Where are you at now?
- Are there any skills you need to develop to be successful?
- What do you think would be the best way for you to acquire those skills?
- What training or work experience would help you be better prepared for this role?

The bottom line is that the most effective method of *counseling* and *coaching* is to ask questions. It allows the people you are mentoring to think for themselves, to be aware of the choices and the consequences for each choice, and then make the decision that is going to give them the best outcomes.

The best way to apply what we have covered in this chapter is to identify two or three things that members of your team do that you would like them to do differently. For example, people arriving late for work or taking extra long breaks outside to smoke. It could be people taking an excessive number of personal phone calls, spending too much time on the phone to friends and family during working hours. Then, choose one or two of those examples and come up with questions that you could ask to get people to:

- Think about their behavior and the *automatic consequences* that follow.
- What impact is their behavior is having on the organization and on other team members, and what are the long term consequences for them personally if they don't change?
- Get their commitment change their behavior.
  Then, put it into practice.

Making Everyone Feel Like an Insider

Another outcome of being the son of Salvation Army missionary parents was that we moved to a new town every six months to two years. As a result, I was the new kid in school many times; by seventh grade, I had attended six different schools! Each time, as the new kid, I was the outsider who had to start from scratch making friends. I knew the drill, but I never got used to it. My transition from eighth to ninth grade was the most awkward. My family moved from a small country town called Warwick, with a population of 10,000 people, to Brisbane, the capital city of the state of Queensland, which had a population of around one million people. On my first day at the state's largest public high school with over 1,300 students, I sat at my desk feeling very much alone.

The teacher introduced me before class as a new student and, as all the students turned to look at me, one face in a sea of faces stood out. He had bright blue eyes, curly red hair, and freckles all over his nose. That red-headed boy's face stood out because he was grinning from ear to ear. At our morning tea break (we have those in Australia), that boy walked straight over to me and introduced himself, "Hey, I'm Don Ross." By day's end we were friends and remained best mates for many years. Frankly, I don't remember anyone else from that class, or even anyone from that school, but I will never forget Don Ross. He made me feel like an *insider* at a time when I felt very much on the outside.

Can you remember a time when you were the new kid at school or the new person at work? What did other people do for you that made you start to feel more welcome?

147

Don made me feel truly accepted for who I was. It was OK just to be myself. I didn't have to try to impress him or be someone I wasn't. In Chapter 3, we looked at the four **Elements of Trust™** that must be present for trust to develop. In this chapter, we are going to explore the element of *acceptance* in more depth—specifically the degree to which you *accept yourself* and the degree to which you *accept others*.

In the book ***I'm OK - You're OK***[14], author Thomas Harris discusses the difference between *OK feelings* and *Not OK feelings*, and how these feelings affect the position from which people live their lives. They are called *life positions*. Yes, the book is several decades old, but to my mind, it remains the most relevant and worthwhile way to understand the feelings you have towards yourself and others. To better understand the different *life positions*, I'll introduce you to five characters: Helen, Jack, Wendy, Mark, and Fred.

HELEN

Helen feels good about herself. She is confident in her opinions and in her ability to express them. This inner appreciation of her own value as a person does not mean Helen feels superior to others. In fact, she is very caring and compassionate, and in her part-time work is a counselor to disadvantaged children. She has a realistic appreciation of her own strengths and uniqueness, and the humility to understand that others have strengths that she does not have.

Most important, she believes she is in charge of her own life, accepts responsibility for her decisions, and trusts herself in her relationships with others. When she performs a task, she is quite objective in measuring how well she did it, and can accept praise or criticism realistically. In social settings, Helen is relaxed and comfortable, not self-conscious, and meets new people with ease. She forms close relationships with others because she believes in herself and does not feel the need to hide her personal quirks. She believes that others like her and is as comfortable in the presence of authority figures, such as the senior executives in her organization, as she is with the frontline workers.

Helen faces problems head-on and takes action to solve them, relying on her inner strength to do so. She sets her own goals and maintains her own standards of behavior rather than doing what is merely expected by others. She feels she is a worthwhile person and is able to handle whatever situations may arise in the future.

JACK

Jack believes he is a worthwhile person. He thinks highly of himself, is confident of his opinions, and doesn't hold back in expressing them to others. What others say and think usually doesn't affect Jack. He is less sensitive to the impact his views have on others than Helen. Jack mostly accepts responsibility for his own decisions and actions, but there are times he blames others for his poor results because of their failure to meet his expectations. When he performs a task, Jack believes he is the best judge of how well it was done. It is what he thinks and feels that counts.

In social settings, Jack is open and comfortable, but he often prefers to be alone rather than in company because most people just don't "measure up" to his standards. His co-workers often see him as manipulative, using people and events to his own gain, particularly with team members reporting to him. Because he perceives himself to be superior to others, he has few close relationships. He is aware of others' hostility and resentment toward him, but their opinions do not concern him. Since others do not have the same qualifications or achievements, their opinions don't count. Jack can be very aggressive and critical.

Jack's strength is his ability to set goals and achieve them. He confronts problems realistically and with purpose, and he feels competent to handle whatever problems come up in the future, except where other people are involved. His confidence in his own ability has made him successful. He finds that others disappoint him often and he feels threatened by not being in control. His manager is aware of the people problems he creates but overlooks them because of the outstanding results he achieves. Deep down, Jack experiences feelings of insecurity and a need to be liked, but he will never share those feelings publicly.

WENDY

Wendy accepts herself for who she is, believes she is a worthwhile person, and accepts responsibility for her own decisions and actions. She is concerned with how others feel about her and is sensitive to criticism. Wendy sees herself as a mentor and likes to help people, especially those not as experienced or as knowledgeable as herself. In fact, she spends quite a bit of time as a manager looking for ways to help people perform better. In social settings, Wendy mostly feels at ease with people, although often she thinks that other people do not have her intellectual capacity. This makes her seem standoffish, distant, or aloof.

Wendy finds few people who "measure up" to her standards. She likes people, but is selective about her relationships, in particular her close circle of friends. Her team members get the impression that Wendy thinks they are incompetent, insignificant, or have something wrong with them. They feel that Wendy does not give them a chance to do things on their own because she is always giving them advice.

Wendy analyzes problems clearly and objectively but rarely seeks input from other team members, preferring instead to make decisions on her own. Her team members often feel like they have no value other than to perform routine tasks and do what they're told. Wendy sees herself as doing the right thing by making the decisions because, after all, she knows more than they do. She feels mentally superior and able to handle the challenges of life as they arise in the future.

MARK

Mark has some difficulty accepting himself as a worthwhile person and feels that others have superior abilities and strengths. He thinks less of himself for it and is seldom confident in his opinions and hesitates before expressing himself. When he feels on sure ground, though, he can express himself quite clearly to others.

To a large extent, Mark does not think he is responsible for the course of his life—circumstances rather than his own decisions have brought him to where he is. He is disturbed by criticism, and finds it difficult to accept praise. It is difficult for Mark to admit he's done a good job or to measure his accomplishments objectively.

Even though he likes people, Mark feels ill at ease in social situations, particularly in the presence of new people, because he is concerned that they will see through his facade. Familiar situations and old friends are more comfortable, therefore he is slow to form close relationships with others. Mark rarely discloses details about himself for fear that he may not be liked. He is mistrustful of strangers and people in general until they prove themselves—and many do not. Authority figures cause Mark a great deal of anxiety. He respects them greatly because of what he sees as their superior capabilities, but he feels uncomfortable in their company and would rather avoid attending meetings or functions with those people because he feels so inadequate around them.

Mark procrastinates when faced with problems and does not have much confidence in his ability to solve them, hoping that if he ignores them they will go away, or that time will take care of it. Mark occasionally finds the strength to better his life, but does so by avoiding conflict. He is very self-conscious, overly concerned by what he imagines others think of him, and does not have confidence in his ability to deal with the future.

FRED

Fred struggles to accept himself as a worthwhile person. He has little confidence in his own abilities and hesitates before expressing himself. Fred believes that circumstances or fate have defined his destiny in life, not himself. He feels his own decisions, when made, have not significantly altered where he is in life, and frequently feels manipulated by others, particularly those who may be perceived as smarter or more powerful. He has difficulty communicating with others because he believes that what he says is not taken seriously. He is not greatly influenced by what others say or think. Fred minimizes his own accomplishments by being very self-critical.

Fred is very selective about with whom he socializes. He finds it difficult to form trusting long-term relationships because he is not comfortable with himself, and he finds it difficult to trust others. Sometimes he finds himself playing roles with others and trying to manipulate them. Fred is not comfortable in the presence of authority figures because he tends to be suspicious of them and their motives.

Fred approaches problems with caution because he lacks the confidence needed to deal with them. He doesn't feel like he has the inner strength to confront them, so he tends to ignore problems, hoping that time or distance will solve them.

Feelings About Yourself

These characters have feelings about themselves and toward others that significantly impact the way they live their lives and the success they've achieved. Let's look at how they feel about themselves. Do they have *OK feelings* or *Not OK feelings*?

One of the best ways to get a good description of *OK feelings* is to observe young children when they're playing. The following feelings come to mind: *happy, relaxed, energetic, confident, curious, adventurous, risk-taking, comfortable, enthusiastic, brave, courageous, excited, exuberant, playful...*

Think about these feelings in relation to yourself. When you are feeling good about yourself, how many of these feelings apply to you?

On the other hand, when you're feeling *Not OK*, in particular *Not OK* about yourself, these are some feelings that come to mind: a*ngry, anxious, depressed, guilty, sick, sad, lonely or just plain upset, apathetic, hopeless, helpless, enraged, afraid, fearful, terrified, threatened, insecure...*

These are not pleasant words. You can even get depressed if you focus on them too long! However, they are feelings that we all experience. Everybody experiences

151

OK feelings and everybody, at times, experiences *Not OK feelings* as well. I want to emphasize that experiencing *Not OK feelings* does not mean that <u>you</u> are *Not OK*, or a bad person. Experiencing *Not OK feelings* is normal, and under certain circumstances, very healthy. It is very normal to feel sad and depressed when you've had a loss. It doesn't feel good, but it's normal and healthy just the same. So when we're talking about *Not OK feelings*, we are talking about feelings that *do not feel OK*.

The more often you experience *OK feelings* about yourself, the more *OK* you will feel as a person. If you genuinely felt these *OK feelings* towards yourself all the time, you'd be very happy to be you. You could look at yourself in the mirror every morning and say, *"I'm OK."* Saying *"I'm OK"* doesn't have anything to do with how you feel about other people. It doesn't mean you are any better or worse than they are. If you think back to our characters, Helen is our best example of someone who believes she is *OK.* Jack and Wendy also operate in a way that indicates that they believe they are *OK.* However, the way they react to and treat other people is very different from Helen. We will understand this difference better after we discuss feelings toward others later in this chapter.

If, on the other hand, you were experiencing the *Not OK feelings* about yourself more often (if most of the time, you felt angry, anxious, depressed, guilty, sick, sad, and lonely), you would not feel too good about who you are. In fact, you would probably come to the conclusion: *"I'm Not OK."* Among our characters, both Mark and Fred have made a decision at some point in life that they are *Not OK.*

There Are Degrees of OK-ness

If you experience *OK feelings* most of the time, you are likely to feel more *OK* about yourself than someone who feels *OK* just some of the time. I use the terms *"I'm very OK"* and *"I'm moderately OK."* It is important to understand here that I am talking about feelings, not facts. When people <u>feel</u> *Not OK*, maybe even believe they are *Not OK*, it does not mean they <u>are</u> *Not OK*, or that others see them as *Not OK.* Their friends and family most likely see them as worthwhile people. We are talking here about self-perception, more specifically *self-acceptance.* How I feel about myself is not necessarily reality. In fact, those who believe they are *Not OK* are often unrealistic in their self-assessment and judge themselves more harshly than other people do. For example, Mark and Fred, who are both operating from a position of *I'm Not OK*, have very little confidence in their ability to control their lives and make effective decisions, yet they hold down jobs, have families who love them, and run their households.

Feelings Toward Others

As indicated earlier, Helen, Jack, and Wendy all see themselves as *OK*, but there are differences in the way they perceive the *OK-ness* of other people. To understand the difference, we need to look at the feelings we have toward other people, again in terms of *OK* and *Not OK*. When you believe that someone else is really *OK*, what are the feelings that you have toward them? The typical *OK feelings* you will experience are: *friendly, trusting, accepting, warm, forgiving, caring, considerate, compassionate, loving…*

On the other hand, if you believe that another person is *Not OK*, then the feelings you may experience towards that person are: a*nger, suspicion, judging, cold, aloof, superior or inferior, disinterested, unforgiving, cynical, uncaring…*

Both Helen and Mark see other people as *OK*. They are more friendly and trusting. But because Mark sees himself as *Not OK*, he feels uncomfortable around new people and is slow to form close relationships. Jack, Wendy, and Fred are all operating from a position that others are *Not OK*, or at least *"Not as OK as me!"*

Think about people you know that fit each of those categories. The person you feel is really *OK* is someone who is very easy for you to relate to. Those that you feel *Not OK feelings* toward are people you have difficulty accepting. We all have a basic belief about people in general. The more you experience *OK feelings* toward other people, the more you believe other people are *OK*. If your basic belief is that other people are *OK*, you believe in the basic goodness of people and that most people are trustworthy.

If, however, you experience *Not OK feelings* toward most of the people you meet (that is, you spend most of your time feeling others are *Not OK*), the more *Not OK* you see other people. If your basic position is that other people are *Not OK*, then you naturally are suspicious of people in general and believe that most people are not trustworthy.

As with self-acceptance, there are degrees to which you accept others. Some people are very trusting of others, even to the point of being gullible and naïve. They believe other people are *Very OK*. At the other end of the spectrum, there are people who don't trust anyone. Because they see others as *Very Not OK*, they tend to be cynical, sarcastic, and judgmental. Where do you see yourself on this scale? Are you more trusting or more skeptical of people generally? This way of looking at people gets a lot more interesting when we look at how these two dimensions of *acceptance of self* and *acceptance of others* affect one another.

If I, I Will

- If I lack trust in myself, I will not trust others.
- If I cannot forgive myself, I will not forgive others.
- If I am dishonest, I will be suspicious of others.
- If I am critical of myself, I will be critical of others.

It makes sense. Your feelings about yourself have a significant impact on the feelings you have toward others. The most striking is: *If I am dishonest, I will be suspicious of others.* But is the reverse true? *If I am suspicious of others, I am dishonest?* We can't be sure. We don't know the whole story—this person may have been taken advantage of many times in his or her life, and may have valid reasons to be suspicious. It does concern me, though, to meet people suspicious of everybody. If they believe everyone is dishonest, I would certainly want to be on my guard.

Looking at this same idea in a positive sense:

- If I forgive myself, I will be forgiving of others.
- If I trust myself, I will be trusting of others.
- If I feel good about myself, I will feel good about others.

This does not mean that if *I trust myself, that I should trust everybody.* That would be foolish. But, if my basic belief is that I am trustworthy, then I would tend to think that most other people are trustworthy as well.

People with high self-esteem, who feel really good about themselves, have absolutely no reason to see other people as less than they are. What does that tell us about people who put others down, who have a need to see others as inferior to themselves? In most cases it's because they have low self-esteem; their superiority is a mask for their poor self-image. They only *feel OK* about themselves when they see themselves as better than other people, so they have to keep on proving they are superior in order to continue to feel temporarily *OK*.

Life Positions

Life positions are the positions in which people live their lives. The four basic *life positions* are:

- I'm OK, You're OK
- I'm OK, You're Not OK
- I'm Not OK, You're OK
- I'm Not OK, You're Not OK

Thomas Harris, in his book ***I'm OK, You're OK***, says all children choose their *life position* by the time they are four years old, deciding at that young age whether they are *OK* or *Not OK*, and whether others are *OK* or *Not OK*[15]. Children are not consciously aware they make this decision, but they do conclude that this is the way the world is for them, accept this as reality, and live their lives from that position until they have the opportunity to change their decision. Change will only happen if we become aware of our beliefs and the position we are operating from, and then have a supportive environment to enable the change. Before you dismiss this idea that people decide their *life position* so young, let's get a better understanding of each of the life positions.

The "OK Corral"

I'M OK, YOU'RE OK = *Get On With*

People operating from the *I'm OK, You're OK* life position *Get On With* life. Helen *gets on with* people, *gets on with* solving problems, and *gets on with* making decisions. She deals with problems when they arise and makes the best decisions she can to move on. She is *self-directed*, taking responsibility for her decisions and actions. She is in charge of her own life and confident in her ability to deal with whatever comes up. Because she is so comfortable in *her own skin*, Helen is not self-absorbed. She is more focused on others than herself, and is very caring and compassionate.

I'M OK, YOU'RE NOT OK = Get Rid Of

People operating from the *I'm OK, You're Not OK* life position have a *Get Rid Of* life approach to whatever is not working for them. In personal relationships, they just *get rid of* their partner. In management roles, when someone performs poorly, they *get rid of* that person. They approach many problems in life this way.

They do not take time to determine the best solutions; it's more important to them to just *get rid of* the problem. It never occurs to them that coaching, mentoring, or training could fix the problem.

There are two kinds of people who operate from this *life position*: those like Jack, who act arrogant, superior, and don't hold back from letting other people know they think they are inferior, and those like Wendy, who continuously need to give their advice on everything.

Jack is the kind of guy you see at a restaurant belittling the staff in a loud voice so other people can hear. What Jack really says is: *"Don't you know how important I am? You're just a nobody!"* It is the *I'm OK, You're Not OK* life position at its worst. If Jack really felt *OK* about himself and believed he was a worthwhile person, would he treat people like that? The answer is no.

The important thing to remember with the *I'm OK, You're Not OK* life position is how they act, not how they feel. In Jack's description, it says he is sometimes insecure and needs to be liked, though he will never share those feelings openly. Underneath it all, Jack really feels *Not OK* about himself and only feels *OK* when he puts himself in a position where he believes he is better than others. Because of this, he has to constantly find fault with other people, point out their weaknesses, and criticize them. The unfortunate thing is that Jack doesn't really understand what he's doing. He truly believes that he is superior; in fact, he has spent his whole life making sure that he is, because that's the only way he can feel *OK* about himself. Because he made the decision as a child to operate from this position, Jack has worked hard to be smarter and better at things than other people so that he has evidence that he is better.

If you have a Jack on your team, your natural instinct may be to bring him down to size. When people act in a superior way, it is only natural that others will try to diminish them or prove to them that they are not superior. Jack thrives on this competition and sees your attempts to diminish him as further proof that you are *Not OK*, and he is. The only way to build an *I'm OK, You're OK* relationship with Jack is to be accepting of him, to look for his strengths and talents, and do what you can to get him to see you as *OK*. You cannot change Jack's *life position*. Only he can do that. But you can change his perception of you by treating him with respect, accepting him, and building trust.

Wendy is a subtler form of the *I'm OK, You're Not OK* life position, called the *Rescuer*. Wendy has low self-esteem and compensates for it by needing to be better than others. But she does like people and needs to be helpful in order to feel *OK* about herself. Wendy is the kind of person who looks over your shoulder while you're working and says, *"Let me show you a better way to do that"* when you didn't really want or need her help in the first place. When she gave up smoking, she had to tell everyone who still smokes, *"You know, you really should give it up."* What Wendy is really saying is: *"I'm OK now, but you're Not OK, because you still smoke. I need to help you with this."* Wendy gets her *OK feelings* about herself by pointing out to others, in a more subtle way than Jack does, that she is better than they. However, this is just a substitute for self-esteem. Like Jack, Wendy is also not aware that she is behaving this way in order to feel *OK* about herself. She truly believes she helps people, and that she has to because they are not as smart as she is.

Getting into an *I'm OK, You're OK* relationship with Wendy may be a little easier than with Jack, but the same rules apply: you need to build trust by being accepting and respectful and appreciating what Wendy's strengths contribute to the team.

I'M NOT OK, YOU'RE OK = *Get Away From*

People like Mark, who operate from the *I'm Not OK, You're OK* life position have a *Get Away From* life approach. Mark sees himself as inferior to others. He often feels embarrassed and uncomfortable around people because he sees them as more capable, important, and valuable than himself. He has difficulty accepting compliments. His usual reply is: *"Oh, it is nothing really. It wasn't that good."* He has difficulty just saying thank you and accepting praise.

When problems arise, Mark avoids dealing with them because he lacks confidence in his own ability to come up with the right solution. Being very self-conscious, he is often concerned other people can see his inadequacies. When I think of people like Mark, I am reminded of a saying I heard years ago: *"We would not worry how much other people thought of us if we realized how little they did."* Isn't that the truth? Mark feels that people are judging him a lot more than they really are.

Getting people like Mark into the *I'm OK, You're OK* life position is much easier than it would be for people like Jack or Wendy because they already see you as *OK*. The challenge is to get them to believe in themselves. Make sure they know you value them as a person and appreciate the contribution they make. When they throw off a compliment with an *Oh, it was nothing*, don't let them get away with it. Respond with: *"No, your contribution is not insignificant. You did do a really good job and I want you to know how much I value having you on the team."*

I'M NOT OK, YOU'RE NOT OK = *Get Nowhere With*

People operating from the *I'm Not OK, You're Not OK* life position have a *Get Nowhere With* life approach. They think: *"If I'm Not OK, and You're Not OK, what's the use?"* Fred, who operates from this position, feels like he's getting nowhere because he has been doing the same thing for so long but makes little progress. Those bursts of optimism he feels when embarking on new projects fade because they never seem to work out. Subconsciously, he tends to sabotage everything he attempts, so Fred gets nowhere solving problems and making decisions. Life seems to keep mundanely going on.

Again, we're talking about how people feel, not about the external reality. People in any of these *life positions* can be very successful outwardly, have lots of talent, and be making a significant contribution. And yet, if they're operating from one of the *Not OK* life positions, they will not be contributing what they're really capable of.

Here's an example: During a weekend personal growth seminar I facilitated, I met the owner of a medium-sized advertising company. This man, Tom, achieved significant success in his life. His business employed close to 200 people, he had a loving wife and two children, and he lived in a large home with a tennis court and swimming pool in one of the most exclusive suburbs in Sydney. But he did not feel good about himself. As we progressed through the weekend, Tom shared with us that both his parents had died when he was little, and he had gone to live with his grandmother who found him to be an interruption to her life and repeatedly told him he would never amount to anything. Tom's drive to succeed was largely driven by his desire to prove his grandmother wrong and amount to something. But when he did, it did not changed how he felt on the inside. Tom realized what he needed to work on was the inside (his beliefs about himself and his worth as a person) not the outside (his wealth and status).

I have talked about these four *life positions* as if they were different kinds of people, and I introduced you to the some characters to help illustrate these positions. However, you can spend time in each of these four *life positions* in any one day. You may have relationships with people on your team that fit each of these four *life positions*. I'm sure you have people on your team that you really like, admire, and respect so you are operating in a *Get On With* life approach with these people. There may also be people on your team you regard as a complete waste of time, have the wrong attitude, are perhaps not totally honest with you and you think there's something wrong with them. You may even want to *Get Rid Of* them. If so, you would be relating to them from an *I'm OK, You're Not OK* life position.

There may be others with whom you feel uncomfortable, who you look at and say, *"Wow, I wish I had what he had"* or *"I wish I could do what she does"* or *"I just feel uncomfortable when I am around him."* You may operate some part of your day from the *Get Away From* life approach. There may be someone who frustrates you because you have tried everything with him or her but to no avail. You feel like a failure because you have worked hard to build a positive relationship and you got nothing in return. You *Get Nowhere With* him and think, *"He's Not OK and, wow, I feel so inadequate when I think about him."*

We all tend to have a home base from which we operate. That is the *life position* we operate from most of the time. Again, you cannot change another person's basic *life position*. Only they can do that. But you can help them to get into a *Get On With* life approach *with you!* The people on your team with whom you already have a *Get On With* relationship are those who are the most engaged, committed to you, and passionate about giving you their best. It would make sense then, to get everyone on your team into a *Get On With* relationship. Only then will everyone feel like an *insider.*

To achieve this, think about how you have operated with each team member in the past. What *life positions* are you operating from with each of your team members and to what extent is what you're doing now influenced by the way you were when you were growing up? If you are going to operate in a *Get On With* way with each of your team members, you have to operate from *I'm OK* to start with. That requires a lot of self-awareness. It requires the willingness to be humble and say, *"I made a mistake. I shouldn't have said that"* or *"I shouldn't have reacted that way"* or *"I'm sorry, that wasn't an appropriate way to say that, let me try that again."* People feel more comfortable when they are with others whom they see as being human, who feel *OK* enough about themselves to admit they made a mistake, and who can apologize and say, *"That wasn't a very good way of handling things."* You can only do that when you know that you are a worthwhile person, and *feel worthwhile* as well. Making mistakes does not change your *worthwhileness.*

An important learning experience that helped me operate more from the *Get On With* life approach was realizing that people who operate from this position are just normal people like you and me. They have bad days, they feel down sometimes, they feel insecure. They find themselves judging people, thinking *"I'm better than them."* But they don't get stuck in those *Not OK feelings.* They are aware of how they are feeling and say to themselves, *"Isn't that interesting. I'm feeling inadequate"* or *"Isn't that interesting, I'm finding fault with that person. Why do I need to do that?"* They know intellectually that they are not inferior or superior, just different, so they let those feelings go. What I used to do was get stuck in the *I'm Not OK* life position not because I <u>was</u> *Not OK*, but because I was <u>feeling</u> *Not OK*. I believed that people who are really *OK* felt *OK* all the time. That's just not true.

When I realized that it was perfectly normal to experience the whole range of feelings from *I'm OK* to *I'm Not OK* and from *You're OK* to *You're Not OK*, I was able to accept that I am still *OK* no matter what I am feeling. I still experience *Not OK feelings*, and it is *OK*. It doesn't feel good, but it also doesn't affect who I am, and I don't let it affect how I feel about myself as a person.

To ensure all your team members feel like *insiders*, they need to know that you believe they are *OK*, that they are worthwhile people, and that they have value to contribute to the team. You can build people up as high as you want to, as long as you're being truthful, realistic, and not artificial. It has no effect on your worth-while-ness. It doesn't take anything away from you because you're *OK*. What can you do with each of your team members to build a *Get On With* relationship?

Conditional vs. Unconditional OK-ness

Another insight that helped me operate in the *Get On With* life mode more of the time was understanding the difference between *conditional* and *unconditional OK-ness*. *Conditional OK-ness* is when we feel *OK* because certain conditions exist. For example, you do a job well and you know it, so you've got this sense of satisfaction. You're feeling good about yourself <u>because</u> you did a great job. That is *conditional OK-ness*. When someone gives you recognition and you feel good about it, that is *conditional OK-ness*. The *OK-ness* is there because you did something. Another example is when you set a goal for yourself in terms of fitness or weight loss, you work at it, you discipline yourself, and you achieve it. You're feeling *OK* <u>because</u> you achieved the goal.

How would you have felt if you had not done the job well and actually made a mistake? Or, if instead of getting recognition for doing a great job, you now get criticism for making a mistake? You might fail to achieve your goals altogether. Of course you would feel a bit disappointed with yourself, but then what? If you really beat yourself up, tell yourself how hopeless you are, and get depressed for a while, your *OK-ness* about yourself is *conditional*. If you admit the mistake, apologize to others if it is appropriate to do so, figure out what you can learn from the experience to do a better job next time, and *Get On With* solving the problem, your *OK-ness* is more *unconditional*.

Unconditional OK-ness is knowing you are *OK*, period. You don't have to do anything or be better than anyone else in order to be an *OK* person. I'm not suggesting that you can do what you like and it doesn't matter. You are still responsible for the consequences of what you do, and you still need to be *self-directed*. Can you look yourself in the mirror in the morning and say, *"You're a really decent, worthwhile person?"* If, when you think about doing that, you feel discomfort in your stomach and that little voice in your mind says, *"Who are you kidding? What about…"* that is a sign the little *Not OK Kid* is still alive and well inside of you.

My little *Not OK Kid* has not gone away, and I don't expect he ever will. And

I'm *OK* with that. When somebody gives me some praise and little *Not OK Keith* inside my head says, *"You're not really that good,"* I know that if I listen to him and let him take control, I will soon be thinking about what was wrong with my performance and getting down on myself. If I try to block out the *Not OK Kid* or deny he's there, I give him more power. Accept your *Not OK Kid*. Whenever your *Not OK Kid* speaks up to deny you feeling good about yourself, just say to yourself, *"Isn't that interesting? There is a part of me that still feels uncomfortable accepting positive feedback."* And remind yourself that you really are *OK, unconditionally!*

Building Your Self-Esteem

Tom, the advertising executive I mentioned earlier, spent his whole life trying to build up his *self-esteem* through qualifications, business success, and accumulation of wealth, but to no avail. Why do so many managers try to build their *self-esteem* by being superior to other people? We see it in people who are leaders of churches, we see it in politicians, we see it in spouses and parents. Some people seem to continually have to remind others they are less *OK*. It may not even be overt or an "in your face way" of putting people down, but more of a subtle little reminder that *"I'm more OK than you are."* Finding fault in others is very common, like the time I was about to point out to my daughter Lauren that she had colored outside the lines. Why would I need to do that if I felt OK about myself?

As a leader, you need each of your team members to be *self-directed*, to become a leader in his or her own right. Your goal is create an environment where that can happen by not promoting a culture of dependence in which people are reliant on you to be the leader all the time. Only when you are operating in the *Get On With* life mode and trust your team to use their talent and be creative, can you get everyone in your team passionate about making your organization the best it can be.

Next, we'll look at how differences between people, or *diversity*, affects the judgments we make about others, and how to get everyone into a *Get On With* life mode.

Diversity

In many ways, I was very fortunate to have an unusual childhood. For the first five years of my life, my family lived in the West Indies, and then lived for two years in Dutch Guiana, which is now called Suriname. The only other children my older brother Kevin and I had to play with were local native children. We were obviously a different color and race, but it meant nothing to me. We went to Sunday school together and played together just like any good friends would. My mother was born in Canada, but lived in India with her missionary parents from age two to fourteen. She returned to India to work as a missionary for many years. Most of her life Mum had been around people who were not Caucasian. It's no surprise one of the things I remember Mum saying often was: *"We're all God's children."*

An interesting aspect of the Salvation Army as a religion is that from its very beginning in the 1800s, women could be ministers—they call them Officers. My mother became a missionary in India on her own before she met my father, who was also a missionary, in Bombay. It worked to their advantage that a Salvation Army officer can only be married to another officer who has been through training college. Growing up, both my parents worked at their missionary roles, although sometimes their roles were quite different. They gave sermons in church, and to us children at home!

I grew up in a home where the woman's role in the marriage was that of a "partner," rather than a "housewife." Unlike many men my age, I wasn't brought up with the traditional belief that the woman's role was restricted to the home—cooking, cleaning, and looking after her husband and children.

Looking at the lack of tolerance and respect between different groups of people today, and the impact that has on the workplace and community, I wonder what beliefs people were taught as children that led them to believe they are superior or inferior to others. Think about the things that have influenced your own beliefs. Consider where you grew up, in what part of town, what part of the country, in what kind of family, your status in the community, your religion, your school, the level of education you attained, and combine that with your life experiences. Then there's who you and your parents are, your gender, your age, your generation, your emotional maturity, and your physical attributes.

Take all of this into consideration and it's no shock that two people who work together side-by-side in the same organization could have different beliefs about a myriad of things. These things can get in the way of mutual understanding and trust. However, it is not the differences between you that cause conflict; it is the belief that *"I am right, they are wrong,"* or *"I am better than them"* that causes it. It is the lack of understanding and acceptance that causes conflict.

The key to making sure that people who are different also feel like *insiders* is to understand and accept them—the foundation of the *Get on With* life position. While it is easier to get into a *Get on With* relationship with someone who is more like you, we need to know how to also *get on with* those who are different. In the **Whole Person Concept**, our needs and values are different. You need to get below the waterline to understand what makes people tick. Only then can you understand and accept them.

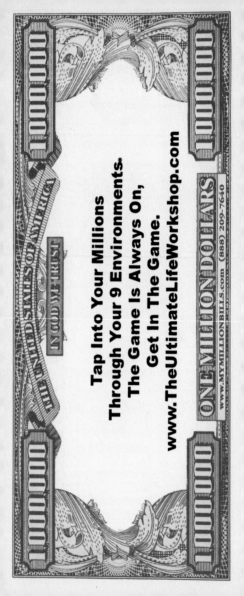

Getting into an *I'm OK, You're OK* or a *Get on With* relationship with someone is a four-step process:

Step 1 – Knowledge: Not knowing about others' backgrounds makes it difficult to for you to understand the way they think, feel, and behave.

Step 2 – Understanding: Awareness of others' needs, values, and life experiences, coupled with empathy for how they think and feel, leads to deeper levels of understanding.

Step 3 – Acceptance: Being *receptive* and curious about others' differences with them helps you to build *respect* for them and to truly value their differences.

Step 4 – Behavioral Skills: How you behave towards people who are different is affected by your *knowledge, understanding,* and *acceptance* of them. Your *interpersonal skills* are a result of your awareness of your behavior, how it affects others, and your ability to adapt the way you relate to each person's uniqueness.

These four steps are the foundation of the **Discovering Diversity Profile*** from Inscape Publishing, Inc., which measures your *knowledge, understanding, acceptance,* and *interpersonal skills* in dealing with people who are different.

KNOWLEDGE

Do you have any team members who are a mystery to you? What do you know about their backgrounds? It's not just getting to know them individually, but also understanding their culture, especially if they are from a different race. Have you tried to learn anything about their culture by reading books or watching related documentaries? You may think you know a lot about it just from having interacted with other people from that culture, but is everything that you've learned really true? Is it possible that some of the things you've learned are stereotypes? A stereotype is a generally accepted belief about a group of people that is not true about that group as a whole.

Here's an example: Several years ago, we did a research study in Australia to identify stereotypes that were barriers to Australians accepting one another and working together effectively. One of the more common stereotypes we found was about our indigenous people, the Australian Aboriginal. The stereotype is that they have a problem with alcohol. Numerous reports in the media about some groups of Aboriginals drinking to excess had reinforced belief in this stereotype.

The research, however, clearly showed that it is not true. Caucasian Australians are more prone to have a problem with alcohol than Aboriginal people. I recall a manager I met at one of my seminars some years ago who argued passionately that this was not a stereotype because of all he had read or heard in the media. He totally dismissed our research.

For those people who want to argue, who strongly believe in a stereotype, I would ask, *"Why is it so important for you to believe that? Why do you need to believe that group of people is inferior?"* If you believe a stereotype to be true, you categorize people as being deficient in some way. They are not as *OK* as you because you don't have those deficiencies. This can lead to you behaving in a diminishing or excluding way toward people who are part of that group.

Here is a challenging exercise for you to do. Take a sheet of paper for each member of your team. Write their name at the top, and what you know about them to be different from you. For example, if you are the opposite gender to them, write that down as a difference. Do the same for differences like race, family background, education, height, weight, age, **DiSC**' behavioral style, and any other differences that come to mind. Now write down any beliefs you have about each difference you have identified. How do these beliefs affect the way you relate toward people from each of these groups? Do any of these beliefs you have make another group inferior in some way? You may think your belief is correct, but what is more important for you as a leader: to be right or to be effective? When everyone on your team feels like an insider and operates in the *Get On With* life position with you, your whole team is more productive and successful. Work through these four steps to better understand how you can develop a plan to *understand, accept,* and *relate* to the people on your team who are different.

Knowledge about them is a critical starting point, and the most accurate way of gaining knowledge about people is to ask them questions like: *"How do you see this situation? Tell me a little bit about your background. What led you to where you are today?"* Obviously, you have to have established a high trust level with people to reach this level of conversation, but if you really want to get to know where people are coming from and truly understand the differences, you have to ask questions.

Here are some questions you could ask to get them talking:

- How do you think our team is performing at present in terms of how well we work together?
- What are your thoughts on how we could improve our teamwork?
- Tell me about what has worked best for you in the past in other teams you have worked with.
- Is there anything you need from me to remove roadblocks that are preventing you from getting your job done?
- What steps do you believe we need to take to be the best we can be?

And if you want them to elaborate a little more on a subject, a great way to do that is simply: *"Tell me more about..."*

UNDERSTANDING

You do not have to have had the same experiences as people to *understand* them. As you listen to what they have experienced and how they see things, use *empathic listening* to tune in to their feelings as well as *comprehensive listening* to understand the factual information they are sharing.

While listening, mentally picture yourself in their situation and imagine, *"If I had been through that, if I was in the same situation as them, how would I be feeling?"* It's not the same as actually being there and feeling it, but having this level of empathy is an important step in beginning to understand them. Your goal is to understand how they see things, and why they respond to certain situations the way they do without judging them.

ACCEPTANCE

Increasing your knowledge of team members who are different and getting to know them so you can understand where they are coming from will help you get into an *I'm OK, You're OK* relationship with them. Acceptance means being non-judgmental of the person; it means believing he or she is basically a good person and intends to do the right thing. In Chapter 1, I described the senior manager who was micromanaging his team because he was operating from an underlying belief that people will do the wrong thing if you don't check on them all the time. When I asked him what he really believed about his people, he realized that he had a great team of people whom he did believe to be trustworthy. He just hadn't thought about it before.

BEHAVIORAL SKILL

This skill allows you to see and relate to people in a way that they feel *I'm OK, You're OK*. By now, you will be able apply much of what you've already read in this book. Take into consideration the other person's **DiSC°** behavioral style, and adapt your behavior to create a more comfortable environment for them. Use the mentoring skills we covered in Chapter 9: adapting your natural *listening approach*, the **Giving** and **Receiving Feedback Models**, and the *coaching* and *counseling* skills. As discussed in the previous chapter, effective mentoring is all about asking the right questions and listening.

I have often wondered how different my first few months would have been at my new high school if Don Ross had not been in my class and made me feel so welcome. What are you going to do to ensure that everyone on your team feels welcome every day? What difference do you think that would make to your team's performance?

CHAPTER

Making Work Meaningful for Everyone

I took my family on a trip to the United States in 1998 for a holiday that included visiting Disney World in Florida. Our daughter, Melissa, was five at the time, so we wanted her to see the famous parade in the Magic Kingdom. We were advised to get to Main Street early to stake out a position, so when we did, we had to wait around for a little while before the parade began. While waiting, a young man dressed in white overalls and obviously a part of the Disney cast came by with a long-handle pan and brush sweeping up rubbish. Passing by us, he saw our little blonde-haired girl sitting on the sidewalk, waiting patiently for the parade to start. He crouched down and started a conversation with Melissa. I don't remember what he said, but she was laughing and having a great time. In the process, a whole group of people around us were also laughing and enjoying the interaction. After a few minutes, he got up and went on his way, continuing to sweep the streets.

The Power of Purpose and Values

I didn't again think about this until some time later when re-reading Jim Collins and Jerry Porras' book ***Built to Last***. As mentioned in Chapter 7, they identify eighteen *visionary* companies that had achieved phenomenal results compared to the *comparison* companies in the same industries. Another primary and distinguishing attribute of each visionary company was that each had established a *core ideology*.[16]

Collins and Porras broke down core ideology into two components:

- **Core Values:** "The organization's essential and enduring tenets—a small set of general guiding principles; not to be confused with specific cultural or operating practices; not to be compromised for financial gain or short-term expediency."

- **Purpose:** "The organization's fundamental reasons for existence beyond just making money—a perpetual guiding star on the horizon; not be confused with specific goals or business strategies."

All eighteen visionary companies not only established their *core ideology*, they also succeeded in having it permeate the entire organization, something the comparison companies had not done.

Disney was one of the visionary companies described in the book. Their *purpose*, as stated in the book, was: "To use our imagination to bring happiness to millions."[17] While reading this in the book, I thought about that young man sweeping up cigarette butts who paused to talk to Melissa. He used his imagination to bring happiness to a little girl and a whole group of people around us. Even though his job could be considered menial work, he knew that he was empowered to use his imagination to make people happy. Now that is a powerful *purpose statement*!

Since the *purpose* of your organization is very reason why it exists, then it makes sense that the better you fulfill that *purpose*, the more successful your organization will be. It also makes sense to create a *purpose statement* everyone is passionate about and committed to fulfilling. In fact, the only reason for having a *purpose statement* is to inspire people to operate by it and to increase the passion and commitment they have for your organization both internally and externally. So if you have a *purpose statement* that doesn't inspire people and fails to clearly state in a few words why your organization exists and how it makes the world a better place for your customers, then it is a waste of time and effort.

Your Organization's Purpose

Why was you organization created and what is its *purpose*? To understand that, look at the relationship between your organization and the external environment. Your organization relates to that environment in two ways:

- **Outputs:** Organizations are created to deliver *output*. Car companies make cars, and an airline is created for the purpose of transporting people from place to place by air. Disney was created to entertain people—that's their *output*.

- **Inputs:** For each organization to be able to deliver *output* to its customers, it needs *input*—customers, suppliers, equipment, facilities and revenue.

This is the same as the **Give-Get Cycle** that I talked about in Chapter 1—your organization was created to *give* something of value to your customers and you obviously need to *get* revenue in order to continue to deliver.

Determining Your Purpose

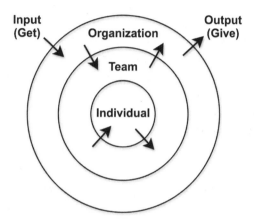

The External Environment

Defining Your Purpose Statement

The Disney Company entertains people. But "We entertain people" is hardly an inspirational *purpose statement* and does not motivate employees to perform at their best. *Purpose statements* should define <u>how</u> you *make the world a better place* for your customers or the community.

Let's look at some examples: Johnson & Johnson provides products and services for the healthcare industry. Stating it like that however, is not very inspirational, so their *purpose statement* is: "We exist to alleviate pain and disease."[18]

The Marriot Hotel Group provides accommodation, restaurants, resorts, and all the other facilities that go with being in the hospitality industry. Their *purpose statement* is: "To make people away from home feel that they're among friends and really wanted."[19]

Having a well articulated and inspirational *purpose statement*, however, is not enough. Everyone in your organization needs to understand how what he or she does contributes to that purpose, just like the young man on Main Street at the Magic Kingdom. You can see in the diagram above that the outer circle is the *organization* that exists in the *external environment* with its outputs and inputs.

Just as each organization is created for a *purpose*, every team within your organization is also created for a purpose—to deliver *output* to the organization. When all the teams in your organization deliver their *output*, your organization is able to fulfill its *purpose*. Each team is composed of individuals who each have a *role,* and each role was created for a *purpose*—to deliver *output* to the team. When each team member fulfills the *purpose* of his or her *role*, the team fulfills its *purpose*. Again, the better your organization fulfills its *purpose,* the more successful your organization will be.

Unfortunately, most organizations define the *output* required from each team and each individual in terms of goals and activities, not in terms of *purpose*. Focusing solely on goals and activities is just as inspirational for the members of your team as defining the purpose of an airline as: "To fly people from point A to point B." If a team and the team members' roles are all created for a *purpose*, then they exist because their *output* contributes to the organization's *purpose*. Doesn't it make sense to clearly articulate what those *purpose*s are?

The Purpose of the Executive Team

Why does your senior team exist? The first answer I usually get from members of a senior team is: *"To make sure we achieve our objectives"* or *"To achieve the bottom line."* My next question is: *"Who achieves the objectives or delivers the results?"* The answer, of course, is the people in the organization who do the work, who produce the products, who make the sales, and who serve the customers so well they come back for more and promote your organization to others.

So if the *purpose* of the senior team is not to produce business results, then what is it? The next most common answer is to control systems and people to ensure they produce the results, and we know that too much control cripples innovation and creativity, and increases bureaucracy. The real reason your organization needs a senior team is that you need a culture that not only allows employees to perform at their best, but that inspires them to be passionate about doing it. The senior team has a significant impact on the culture of your organization—and they should. A very important part of their *purpose* is: *To create a work environment where everyone in the organization wants to and can perform at his or her best.*

A Purpose-Centered Approach to Work

In the book **Intrinsic Motivation at Work**, author Kenneth W. Thomas[20] describes the power of having a *purpose-centered* approach to work. For example, what is the *purpose* of a flight attendant's role on a commercial airline? If you think about why they are there, the first thing that comes to mind is safety. In the event of an emergency, they can ensure that all the correct procedures are followed and all passengers will be safe. But there is more to their role than safety. Flight attendants also provide service on a normal flight; they make the trip as safe, comfortable, and enjoyable as they possibly can. Obviously, the more comfortable and enjoyable each flight is for you, the more likely you will fly with that same airline again, and recommend it to friends and colleagues.

How comfortable and enjoyable have your recent flights been? On almost all the flights you have been on lately, you have felt safe. Not necessarily because of the flight attendants, but because there was no emergency. But what have the flight attendants done to make sure you were comfortable and happy? Have you had a number of flight attendants who seemed to have no concern for your comfort or enjoyment? If that is the case, they fail in this area because they do not see that as part of the *purpose* of their *role*. They are focused more on the activities and the tasks they are assigned to perform, rather than focusing on the passengers' satisfaction.

When employees are focused on the activities and tasks for which they are responsible, they often lose sight of the *purpose* of why they are performing those tasks; in other words, they become *activity-centered* rather than *purpose-centered*. The *activity-centered* flight attendant focuses on doing the tasks that are required at various stages of the flight: the before take-off checklists, safety briefings, serving refreshments, collecting rubbish, and so on. Typically, there is no focus on you, the passenger.

Sometimes you get a *purpose-centered* flight attendant who understands that the purpose of her role is more than safety and basic service. She will smile at you, interact with you, check on you to see if you need a pillow—basically go around the airplane and make sure people are happy. The *purpose-centered* flight attendant performs all the same tasks as the *activity-centered* attendant, but those tasks are just a part of what she does to fulfill the *purpose* of her *role*. Her focus is primarily on you, the passenger, and your satisfaction.

If you have traveled on Southwest Airlines recently, you would know the difference I'm talking about. Not only is the Southwest Airlines executive team focused on the *purpose* and *values* by which they operate, they have empowered every employee to use his or her imagination and creativity to make each trip as much fun as possible for you. It is no surprise that Southwest Airlines is the most financially successful airline, remaining profitable right through the period of time post-September 11, 2001, the oil crisis, and all the other recent challenges that have sent other airlines into Chapter 11 protection. And they have not had to lay off a single employee to achieve this success. Why? A significant part of it is that they are *purpose-centered*.

When people are *purpose-centered,* they are focused on doing whatever needs to be done to achieve that purpose. They are not limited by a set of procedures or a series of tasks to perform. Therefore, a *purpose-centered* approach will produce far greater results then just focusing on activities.

You know from your own experience the difference between a *purpose-centered* server in a restaurant, and one who is *activity-centered.* The *purpose-centered* person is focused on your satisfaction. The *activity-centered* person is focused on taking your order and delivering your food and drinks, and, if you're lucky, doing it in a timely manner.

What difference would it make in your team, or in the whole organization, if all employees knew what the *purpose* of their jobs were and were focused each day on making sure that everything they did was done with their *purpose* in mind? How would that impact on your organization's results?

Intrinsic Motivation

What's the most rewarding aspect of your work? Is it creating new products, ideas, or systems that provide value for other people? Is it seeing your customers benefit from the products and services you sell? Is it mentoring people within your organization and seeing them grow as individuals? These are *intrinsic* rewards because they come from inside of you. They are beyond *extrinsic* rewards, like bonuses, pay raises, commissions, share options, etc.

Another valuable concept noted in the book ***Intrinsic Motivation at Work*** is how powerful *intrinsic motivators* can be compared to *extrinsic motivators.* I'm not suggesting that you don't need or should not use *extrinsic* rewards. They are an important part of any organization's reward and recognition program. It seems to me, though, that most organizations focus exclusively on *extrinsic* rewards (which cost more) and lose out on the power of *intrinsic* rewards to increase engagement and commitment. Thomas describes four **Intrinsic Rewards**[21] that significantly increase a person's motivation, commitment, and passion within the organization:

- A Sense of Meaning
- A Sense of Choice
- A Sense of Competence
- A Sense of Progress

A SENSE OF MEANING

Remember the young man sweeping up cigarette butts at Disney World? His work is meaningful to Disney, because he is keeping the streets clean and the environment healthier. But that man was also passionate about his *organization's purpose* of making people happy. Using his imagination made his contribution to the organization more valuable, and it increased the satisfaction and fun that he got out of his job.

A *sense of meaning* is strongly influenced by *purpose*. When people understand the *purpose* of their *role* and how it contributes to the *purpose* of the team and the organization, their work is more meaningful. They know what they do is significant, even if they are working on a production line operating a machine and cannot see the customers. They know that what they're making, or the component they're making is significant because they believe in their product and know that it makes a real difference to the people who buy it.

To achieve this *purpose-centered* approach in your organization, it is important to not only establish your organization, team, and individual purposes, but to also have regular conversations about them. You need to have regular team meetings where you discuss how well you are fulfilling your *purpose*.

Core Values also increase a sense of meaning—we covered this topic extensively in Chapter 7. Now you see how important it is for people to know that they are working for an organization that is honest, ethical, and has high standards. When employees know that they are being fully supported from the CEO down, to operate by your *core values* for quality, customer focus, innovation, teamwork, etc., they have a greater sense of pride in your organization and what it stands for.

A SENSE OF CHOICE

We know when employees feel they have no choice, they will *comply* or *rebel*. *Self-directed* people cannot operate in an environment where they have no choice because the basic belief of the *self-directed* person is: *I always have a choice.* If you give them no choice, they will choose anyway—*to leave*!

Giving people a sense of choice means letting them have a say in how things are done and some input into the goals you want to achieve. You don't always have a choice about organizational goals and objectives, so sometimes your team goals are also predefined. What choice you do have is usually in terms of how you will achieve your goals. When you know what the *purpose* of your team is (what output is required), there may be a better way of achieving your *purpose,* or even exceeding the output expectation. By giving people who are performing the roles more say in how they can improve performance, or reduce waste or cost, you not only increase performance, you have increased the motivation and commitment of your team. When you give people a *sense of choice*, they know you trust them, they make more of a contribution, and their passion for what they do ignites like a wildfire.

A SENSE OF COMPETENCE

When do you feel the most *competent* at work? Is it when you are using your talent and skills to do something at which you excel? Some people feel most *competent* when they are overcoming challenges or solving problems. For others, it's when they are energizing others and getting the best performance out of their team. What we've been talking about in this book will help your team develop a *sense of competence,* but the most relevant skills we have covered are those related to mentoring. In the next chapter, we are going to look at *Creating a High-Performance Team.* Your focus will switch from thinking about each of your team members as individuals to thinking about how to transform your group of people into a *winning team.*

People naturally need to learn and grow. As a leader, it makes sense to see that as a primary part of your role. Are you constantly looking for opportunities to help people learn and grow, and increase their *sense of competence*? In addition to what they can learn on the job and from your mentoring, what training or education would help them develop their skills and knowledge and become a more productive team member? One of the things organizations do to get extraordinary performance out of ordinary people is to invest in people. You cannot get the best performance out of people if you do not invest time and money in their development.

A SENSE OF PROGRESS

When we talk about a *sense of progress*, there is, obviously, some form of measurement involved. From my observations, most organizations' measurements are determined by management. When employees have no say in the goals that are set for them or how their performance will be measured, you get *other-directed* behavior and no accountability. Some people will comply, grudgingly, with the directive, and have no real commitment to achieving it; others will rebel and make sure you don't achieve the goal. Building a *high-performance team* requires you allow team members a say in how they'll be measured. You need to give your team a voice.

Many managers believe if they let employees set their own goals, they will set them too low, and the organization will not achieve the best results. The research does not support that thinking, and, as I have mentioned earlier, our own research has shown that people really do want to perform at their best. Many organizations are finding that when employees set their own performance goals, they set them higher than management could ever have set them.

Here's an example: An organization in Delaware has a call center that provides technical assistance to their customers who use this organization's diagnostic equipment and supplies to perform pathology tests. In 1999, a newly appointed vice president in charge of that business unit was alarmed to discover that this call center was in last position in the industry for customer satisfaction. Scores were below 50 percent in all five areas that were being measured. Obviously, if you are last in customer satisfaction, that is costing you business.

In addition to providing customer service training for the customer service representatives, Integro's leadership development process was implemented with the management team to create a work environment where employees would be more *engaged*, more *self-directed*, and *take responsibility* for increasing customer satisfaction. About a year into the process, when customer satisfaction numbers had started to improve and employees were getting more engaged, the vice president asked employees what they thought they could achieve in terms of customer satisfaction. After some discussion, team members came back with a target of 96 percent, a score that would put them at the top of the industry. Although the management team thought they were aiming too high, especially considering where they had come from, the employees were confident they could achieve it.

Not only did they achieve their goal across all five areas within the next eighteen months, by the end of 2002, they had exceeded it, achieving a 98 percent average. Since then, they have achieved an average score of 100 percent many times. What made the difference was that *employees owned the goal*. They were their numbers. Every month when the research company delivers the report, the customer service representatives are as anxious to see the results as the managers. If they drop below 100 percent, they discuss amongst themselves the problems that have occurred and any customer complaints that have been received to determine how to get back to 100 percent.

When employees have input into the goals and determine how they're going to be measured, they set the bar higher than management could dare. These four *intrinsic motivators* really ramp up the level of engagement and increase the passion team members have for what they do by making their work so meaningful that they love coming to work every day.

CHAPTER

Building High-Performance Teams

In 1995, the CEO of an Australian company asked me to facilitate a strategic planning retreat with his executive team. The CEO's stated objective was to establish the organization's new vision and he wanted to get his team members' commitment to support it. He had communicated his commitment to creating a work culture based on teamwork and empowerment to his entire organization before the retreat. Among those changes was an "E" to precede each business unit (BU) to become an EBU, or *Empowered Business Unit*. Each EBU leader was asked to develop a strategic plan and submit it to the CEO for review. Well, review often became revision by the CEO, without the EBU leader's knowledge or consent. The CEO also revised sales targets and sent the reports back to the EBU leaders. So much for being *empowered!*

The CEO had not revealed to anyone prior to the strategic planning meeting that his "vision" for the organization was to double sales from $500 million to $1 billion in three years. When he did reveal it during the session, it shocked the rest of the team. Only an aggressive acquisition program could achieve that result, and it would divert energy and financial resources away from key business objectives.

The first problem was that the CEO's "vision" was not a vision. It was a goal. Financial numbers do not make a vision. What does a billion-dollar company look like? What does a 20 percent increase in market share look like? A *vision* is a well-articulated picture of what the organization will look like at a point in time in the future: what the organization will be doing, what the community and the press will be saying about it, and how the organization will fulfill its purpose. The CEO's one billion dollar "vision" did none of this.

Second, no one on the senior team saw that goal as being realistic or even desirable because of the diverted energy and effect on primary business goals. Without team effort, there was no team commitment. The CEO was not honest with me about his initial desire, which was to get me to influence the team to *comply with* his autocratic goal. The heated argument that ensued about the CEO's "vision" resulted in the alienation of most of his senior team; there had been no open discussion or opportunity for them to put forward an alternative view. The session failed to achieve his objective, and four members of his executive team resigned within the next few weeks, because they realized their input was not required or valued.

This CEO had surrounded himself with experienced and intelligent people who could have provided valuable insight to help the organization achieve its potential. But he was so locked in to his own personal ambitions for the organization—which by the way, were subsequently not achieved—that he never thought to ask. In fact, his aggressive acquisition program resulted in a significant reduction in the organization's stock price.

When Is a Team Not a Team?

Just as the Empowered Business Units in this organization were not empowered, the senior executive team was not a real team. A group of people that calls itself a team and does not do what real teams do is not a team!

A real team is a group of people who are very clear about and approve of their *purpose, values, vision, goals, procedures,* and *roles*. That's not all. Real teams fulfill their *purpose,* adhere to their values, and achieve their vision. Team members understand the *purpose* of the team is to deliver output to the organization that makes a difference, so they focus on being accountable for delivering those results.

In the book *The Wisdom of Teams*, authors Jon R. Katzenbach and Douglas K. Smith describe a *high-performance team* as: "a group that meets all the conditions of real teams and has members who are also deeply committed to one another's personal growth and success."[22] In *high-performing teams*, each member genuinely cares about each other's success and fosters team spirit.

A sport I really enjoyed playing in high school was Rugby Union. I was a sprinter on the track team, so I played on the wing, which meant that my teammates would pass the ball out wide to me and I would "fly" down the field to score. In eleventh grade, our team went the entire season undefeated, playing all the top rugby schools in Brisbane. It was very rare for any team to do that, and still is today. How we won is what I am most proud of about that team. Our team did not have superstars—at least not anyone who went on to play for the Australian Wallabies—but we worked very well together as a team. As the season progressed, we came to rely on each other more, move the ball around more quickly and skillfully, and literally run rings around the opposition. We were passionate not just about playing, but also about training. We all gave our best and the coach really worked us hard. We also had a lot of fun. It stands out for me as a time when I experienced the passion of being on a *winning team*.

Increasing Your Odds

In ***Increasing the Odds for High-Performance Teams: Lessons Learned***, by Arlen Leholm and Raymond Vlasin[23], five diverse case studies were presented to clearly show how a *high-performance team* can be made in any environment where teamwork is required. At one end of the spectrum, the authors share how both management and labor leaders at a Quaker Oats plant created a *high-performance team* at the top to overcome production problems in a manufacturing plant. In a completely different environment, Leholm and Vlasin reported on a *high-performance team* with a Women's Interest Group in a poor village in India whose purpose was to overcome poverty and illiteracy and improve their agricultural skills and techniques. Some of the key lessons learned from their research are:

- It is imperative to start with an assessment of where the team and the organization are, not where you want them to be.
- A strong focus on performance is central to the *high-performing teams*.
- Professional development of all team members appears vital to creative and innovative actions and enhanced performance.
- Establishing and fostering a trust environment is fundamental, if not crucial, to the formation and successful operation of *self-directed* teams.
- *Empowerment* of teams is vital to achieve high-performance.

The wonderful people at Integro are also an excellent example of a *high-performance team* with a great team spirit. Of course, I am a little biased, but expanding to the United States would not have been possible without their support, commitment, and outstanding results. It has helped me to learn that I am not *indispensable*. At Integro, we are not immune to some of the same problems that occur in any workplace, but we'd like to think—and we do have a lot of evidence—that we are equipped with the *awareness* to deal with problems as they arise in the ways I've talked about so far in this book.

Steps to Building a High-Performance Team

Before a *high-performance team* can be created, all team members must want to play, and play at the top of their game. In the Introduction, I described the **Passion Pyramid™,** which shows the first four levels of need that must be satisfied *before* people to will want to play on a *winning team.* Just to remind you, they are:

- Level 1 – Their *need for respect* is being met
- Level 2 – They have the opportunity to *learn and grow* every day
- Level 3 – They feel like an *insider*
- Level 4 – They know their work is *meaningful*

If someone remains dispirited or not motivated, identify which of these needs are not being met, and go back to that level with him or her. If you don't do that, they will hold back the performance of the rest of the team until their needs are met. Presuming everyone on your team wants to play at the top of his or her game, then you must focus on the steps required to create a real team, where team members are very clear about and agree with the team's *purpose, values, vision, goals, procedures,* and *roles.*

Team Alignment

Step 1: As a team, clarify and agree on your *purpose.* Success may be measured financially, but your team's *goal* should be focused on the *output* they need to deliver to ensure the goal is achieved. My winning rugby team was not focused on winning. We were focused on the only output we could control: our individual and team performance. We knew when we used the talents of each team member, when they were most needed *(shared leadership),* we got the best results. What is the *output* that your team needs to focus on?

Step 2: As a team, clarify and agree on the *values* your team must operate by to be successful. In Chapter 7, we looked at two sets of values: your organization or team's *core values* and the **Values That Build Trust™.** Ask your team how well they think they are performing against these standards, and what they can do to improve: *"What difference would it make in our team if we all operated by our core values and the values that build trust every day? Are we committed to acting by them on a daily basis?"* Then identify specific behavioral guidelines for each value that every team member is willing to commit to. These guidelines become your team's *code of ethics* or *code of conduct, "the way we do things around here."*

Step 3: Before you go any further, ensure you have the *right people on the bus* and the *right people in the right seats.* As we've discussed earlier, being a *right person* is more to do with the person's values and commitment than it is to do with talent or skill, but whether he or she is in the *right seat* has a lot to do with talent.

Team Talents

I have always been a "dreamer." My mind wanders off onto ideas of how things could be. Growing up, I'd get into trouble for day-dreaming and I never really outgrew it. Since I took over Integro, I've had a never-ending supply of ideas on how we can improve our products and how we can market them. Some of my ideas did not work. Some even failed miserably, but that has not prevented me from coming up with new ideas or using other people who are much better at thinking through ideas than I to help shape them. I used to think people who poked holes in my ideas were negative people who derived pleasure from poking holes. Now I know from experience that many of my ideas did have holes in them and that my team was mostly trying to help. The **Team Dimensions Profile,** another of Inscape Publishing's valuable learning instruments, showed me that I have a talent for *possibilities*—I never have had a problem coming up with ideas about how things could be. It also helped me to understand that I lacked other talents, especially when it came to turning ideas into a winning plan. I need others on my team whose talents compliment my own.

This profile does not measure your behavioral style or personality; rather, it measures how you think and behave when working with others to accomplish a specific purpose. Underpinning this model are two basic dimensions:

- A talent for *possibilities* or *realities*
- A talent for *interaction* or *analysis*

Are you consistently thinking about the *possibilities* of what could be achieved? Or are you more in tune with the *realities* of what you are facing on a day-to-day basis? Do you have a talent for *interaction*, for tuning into others' feelings and building relationships? Or do you have more of a talent for *analysis* with a logical, questioning mind and pride yourself on your objectivity?

For me, I am strongest in *possibilities,* with a secondary talent for *interaction* and lack in *realities* and *analysis.* That is why I have implemented unrealistic or only half-developed ideas in the past. But I know this now, and I make sure that someone else on our team is able to take over the leadership of those parts of our planning and execution, which he or she is much more talented in.

Understanding Team Conflicts

Potential *team conflicts* occur between the opposite ends of each dimension. Those with a talent for *possibilities* are conceptual thinkers, imaginative, and good at seeing the master plan. Contrast that with team members who have a talent for *realities,* who are more practical and systematic, have a structured approach to things, and are more focused on the *details* than the *master plan.* They may see people with a talent for *possibilities* as unrealistic, impractical people who are *off with the fairies!* And vice versa, be seen by those with a talent for *possibilities* as rigid, unimaginative people who are *stuck in the mud!*

Awareness is crucial here, not just to minimize unproductive conflict, but also to ensure that you capitalize on the strengths of each team member to avoid the pitfalls associated with a lack of any one of the team talents. When a team talent is absent, this is what happens:

- A talent for *possibilities* is the *Creator* role. When missing, there are no new ideas.
- A talent for *interaction* is the *Advancer* role. When missing, implementation tends to stall.
- A talent for *analysis* is the *Refiner* role. When missing, new ideas are not thought through or details are overlooked.
- A talent for *realities* is the *Executor* role. When missing, either nothing is implemented or it is not followed through to completion.
- A combination of all four talents is the *Flexor* role. When missing, it can lead to stress and conflict between the other roles.

When you think about each of the four primary roles, *Creator, Advancer, Refiner* and *Executor,* they form a logical sequence. When a problem arises or you have a need to develop a new system or process, you need *Creators* who can see the *possibilities* to start generating ideas. Then you need *Advancers* who are receptive to new ideas to choose the best ones and use their talent for *interaction* to gain support for the idea. The next stage is to get the *Refiners* to use their talent for *analysis* to test out the idea, check for "holes", and develop a plan that is actually going to work. Finally, you need *Executors* to use their talent for *realities* to follow through and implement the plan and stay on course, making sure that you achieve the end result, and to report back on what actually happened.

The Z-Process

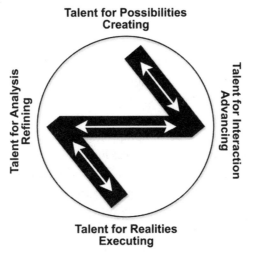

Talent for Possibilities
Creating

Talent for Analysis
Refining

Talent for Interaction
Advancing

Talent for Realities
Executing

The Z-Process

Turning ideas into successful outcomes by using the talents of all your team members is called the *Z-Process*. The value of the **Team Dimensions Profile** is that it helps team members identify where they can contribute most strongly in this *Z-Process*. There are two benefits of this awareness:

- Team members who know they have a talent that other team members do not possess recognize that they have a responsibility to step forward and provide leadership in their area of strength.
- Knowing the *team talents* of other team members helps each team member, including the appointed leader, understand when he or she needs to step aside and let others take the lead.

When Your Team Is Out of Balance

What happens when your team does not have a balance of each of the *team talents*? In an IT company in Sydney, we found that the technology department was experiencing a significant increase in customer complaints soon after the company had developed a very sophisticated database program for large financial institutions. The technology department was responsible for developing the software, customizing it for each customer, and integrating new developments and recommendations from their customers' experiences.

The majority of the increased customer complaints were due to bugs in the software, as well as specific design requests not performing up to the clients' expectations. When we identified the team talents, we found absolutely no *Advancers* with a talent for *interaction* and only one *Refiner* with a talent for *analysis*. All three people in a management role were *Creators*, with a talent for *possibilities*, and all of the program analysts who wrote the code were *Executors* with a talent for *realities*. When a job came in from a client, the *Creators* would get together and discuss it, come up with ideas, draft up an outline of what the client wanted, call in the programmers (*Executors*), and communicate to the programmers what the client wanted, and then the programmers would go and start writing the code.

When the team saw the team composite report, they all started laughing, saying that they could see exactly what was happening: "We end up with all these bugs, and the client sends it back and wants it rewritten because it doesn't do what they asked for." With no one in the *Advancer* role to choose the best ideas or to ensure that the communication between other team members was effective, the *Refiner* role was being overlooked, even though they had one team member who was a *Refiner*.

Because the managers lacked the talent for *analysis,* they did not appreciate the *Refiner's* potential value to the team. I took them through a series of activities to learn how to implement each step in the *Z-Process* and, as a result, work quality improved significantly. They saved more time, reduced wasted effort, and created more satisfied clients.

Getting the Right People in the Right Seats

Think about each role on your team. Are there things team members are required to do that they do not have the talent for? And are there other team members who do have the talent for that work who would love to take it over? Remember, people enjoy doing things they're good at. It seems effortless to them, but it's hard work to the person who lacks the talent. It's time to rethink this outdated idea of fitting people into jobs, trying to put square pegs in round holes, and creating jobs for people. The **Team Dimensions Profile** shows how team members' talents can be best applied in their current roles and reveals what causes them stress (i.e. what skills are outside their range of flexibility). Through it, you can redesign jobs or roles where possible so that you really capitalize on the strengths and talents of your existing team members. Your team members' expectations will be better met by allowing them to stretch out of their comfort zone to perform the tasks required.

Back to the Steps

I interrupted the steps to building a *high-performance team* to introduce you to the **Team Dimensions Profile** and the *Z-Process*, because I have found those tools very effective for guiding teams through the remaining steps and achieving the end result: becoming a *high-performance team*. Let's get back on track…

Step 4: Establishing a *Shared Vision*. Where do you want to be in two, three, or five years from now? Get the team to choose the timeframe and start brainstorming. What will this team be doing at that time in the future, what will it have achieved, what will members of the team be saying? How will the rest of the organization and your clients react to your team's achievements? Have your team craft their *vision statement* by answering the following questions about the team as if you are at that point in time in the future, and write it in the present tense:

- Who are we?
- What do we do?
- How do we do it?

For example, this is the *vision statement* the team of software developers came up with:

"We are a team of innovative, dynamic software developers who create state-of-the-art financial software solutions. We achieve this by:

- Utilizing the talents of all team members
- Exceeding our customers' expectations
- Continuously improving our products"

Step 5: Agreeing on *mutual goals*. Once you have clarity and approval from all team members for your vision, have them identify the things you are going to have to accomplish to make that vision real. Whose support will you need and how will you get it? List all of the goals that must be achieved, then prioritize them in order of importance by getting the group to vote for their top three to five goals. The rest of the goals still have to be achieved; you just want to ensure you start on the most important things first.

This is where many teams get stuck. While doing a strategic planning session with the senior executive team of an international distribution company, I included the **Team Dimensions Profile** to make the best use of each team member's talents during the process. Soon after I had handed out the profiles to each of them and given them some time to read them, I noticed three of the team members get up and meet together in a corner. They started looking at each other's profiles, and soon burst into laughter. I wandered over to where they were to see what was so funny, and they were quite eager to share it with me. There was nothing funny about their profiles; all three of them had scored quite strongly in the *Creator* role, with a talent for *possibilities*. What *was* funny was that the three of them were a sub-group who had taken responsibility for a new project six months ago, and despite numerous meetings between them since, they still did not have a plan. They did not have the talents for *analysis* or *realities* to assist in developing a plan and executing it.

Step 6: Formulating a *strategy*. The following points focus on how to keep all team members involved and contributing at this part of the *Z-Process*. One of the reasons many teams do not complete their action plans or execute them is because the *Creators* and *Advancers* lose interest at this stage.

Ask one team member to volunteer to take responsibility for each of the three to five goals you will work on initially. If you have a small team, start with three; a larger team, four or five goals. Then ask other team members to sign up for the goal they wish to work on so that everyone is involved in one of the sub-teams. Ideally, you want a *Refiner* and *Executor* on each sub-team, but if you don't have them, explore ways of recruiting people with these talents from outside the team to help with the development of the plan and with execution.

Get each group to write on index cards or sticky notes, one idea per page, everything they can think of that must be done to achieve their goal. Everyone should participate, and it does not have to be structured. It's brainstorming. Even though we are now in the *refining* stage of the *Z-Process*, the *Creators* and *Advancers* can get involved because you are using a more *creative* and *interactive* method of developing action ideas. The remaining steps can be done as part of a team meeting, or have each sub-team find their own time and place to meet and report back to the whole team at the next meeting.

Once all ideas have been generated, get each sub-team to sort their action ideas into chronological order—what must be done first, then next, etc. Finally, determine who will be responsible for each action item and by what date and time it is to be completed.

Step 7: Ensure *execution* of the strategy. *Executors,* with their talent for *realities,* should take the lead here. This does not necessarily mean everyone else should go away and leave it to them. Even if much of the *execution* phase is best done by team members with a talent for *realities*, you want all team members to stay committed to the goals and be willing to do whatever it takes to achieve them. You complete this step by asking each team member for that *commitment* to *mutual accountability* for achieving the outcome. That's what *self-directed* people do.

Step 8: Continuous improvement through *shared leadership*. In Chapter 1, we discovered that *leadership is an <u>act</u>, not a role*. The final step in building a *high-performance team* is to get the team to take ownership of continually improving their own performance. The *Out-In-Out* process is the key to that. You see something *Out* there that needs to be changed, fixed, or improved. You go *In* to process your thoughts, feelings, and observations and make choices about what can be done to change, fix, or improve what you've noticed. Then you act *Out* your decision to change, fix, or improve it.

By now, everyone on your team should be very aware of what is working and what is not. Your team should also understand that each of them brings different strengths and talents to the team and, as a result, each sees things that other team members don't see. You want each team member to accept responsibility for communicating to the team the things he or she is seeing that need to be changed, fixed, or improved. Even if that team member thinks everyone else should be able to see it, if no one has spoken up, it is his or her responsibility to speak up, even if he or she thinks the thoughts or observations may be unpopular. That is another important message in ***Increasing the Odds for High-Performance Teams*** by Arlen Leholm and Ray Vlasin: "One of the important elements to fostering success in high-performance teams is the positive treatment of divergent views and approaches."[24]

Every few months, have a team meeting that is specifically focused on the things team members see that need to be changed, fixed, or improved in order to improve performance. Collect all ideas without judgment, and sort them into two categories: *simple* or *complex*.

Simple problems call for *simple* solutions and generally do not require significant investments of money, time, or other resources. Some people call this the *low hanging fruit*—they are easily picked. Quickly learn what went wrong and plan steps to make it right in the future. Ask for a meeting and deal with it. No in-depth problem solving or investment required.

Complex problems are identifiable but require research to solve and implement the solution. Once your team knows how to use the *Z-Process* and a complex problem is identified, put together a task team with a balance of *team talents*, and get them to work through the *Z-Process* to come up with a plan to fix it.

Being a Resource to Your Team

Your involvement in this process is only needed if the team wants your input as a *resource*. Don't interject—ask them if they need it, or you'll risk lapsing back into being the *authority*. You want them to take ownership and be committed to the outcome, so be a mentor and use questions to help them discover the answers for themselves. That does not mean that you should never give advice. There will be times when your knowledge and experience is needed by the team, but it is best given when they *ask* for it. Many leaders fear that if they are not leading the team or sharing their knowledge and experience whenever they can, they won't be needed anymore and will become redundant. It's no wonder that many managers have difficulty letting go of some level of control.

This fear is imagined rather than real. Think about it this way: If you have coached and mentored your team to becoming a *high-performance team*, don't you think they would have a very high level of respect for you? They will value your experience and insights; of course they will ask for your input.

Also, how many leaders do you know who have the ability to turn a group of not very engaged employees into a *passionate, high-performance team?* There are very few. When you apply the skills described in this book, your leadership talents will be in very high demand.

But the entire process, that of transcending from being a manager with a group of averagely engaged employees to becoming a leader of a *passionate, high-performance team*, begins with you.

In the monograph ***Good to Great and the Social Sectors***, Jim Collins says, "Mediocre companies rarely display the relentless culture of discipline—disciplined people who engage in disciplined thought and who take disciplined action—that we find in truly great companies."[25]

Relentless discipline created a great company, and a great leader. Leaders fail to deliver on their team's potential because they won't do the things they must do to achieve that success. There is no way around it. You cannot achieve what your organization is capable of without the passionate support of some very talented people. You also cannot do it with people who are switched off while they're at work. Every leader in your organization needs the skills described in this book if you are going to bring out the best in all your employees and light that fire of passion in their bellies. They don't just need the skills; you also need to create that *culture of discipline*, starting with yourself.

Do you have the courage and commitment to do what it takes? No excuses. No ifs, buts, or maybes; either you are going to do it, or you're not. I would like to share one last thing with you: six *guiding principles* that Ralph Colby shared with me when I first joined Integro that have helped me stay the course. Some people have called them *six crazy ideas*, but I think they will make a lot of sense to you now that you have read this book. I have listed the principles first, followed by further explanation.

1. **The truth about myself will set me free.**
2. **I have created myself.**
3. **I am responsible for myself.**
4. **The past does not control me.**
5. **There is nothing to be afraid of.**
6. **The answers are within me.**

1. **The truth about myself will set me free.** The real challenge throughout this book has been for you to develop *self-awareness* and be honest with yourself about a lot of things. Why do you want to be a leader? What do you have to *give* that is of value to others, in order to *get* the rewards you expect from being a leader? Knowing the *truth* about your behavioral style and the impact you have on the environment you create gives you the *freedom* to adapt your behavior and create an environment in which people love coming to work and want to perform at their best. Knowing the *truth* about the way you most naturally listen makes you *free* to adapt your listening approach to mentor people and bring out their best.

You were challenged to be truthful about which *life Position* you operate from most of the time and to look at your relationships with the important people in your life—your team members and members of your family. Once you know this *truth* about yourself, you are *free* to choose the *I'm OK, You're OK* or *Get On With* life position. Once you know the *truth,* which is that you created the environment where people are more *compliant* and *rebellious* than *self-directed,* you are *free* to change the environment. If you don't accept these truths about yourself, then you will keep on doing what you have always done. Just don't expect a different result, either for you or for your company's bottom line.

2. **I have created myself.** Your parents had something to do with it, but who you are today is more to do with you than anyone else. Everything you have done throughout your life, every decision you've made, and every action you've taken has created the person that you are today. You might not have chosen the cards that life dealt you, but you did decide how to play them. The circumstances in your life have not made you who you are—how you dealt with them did. The other big insight I got from this principle was that if *I have created myself,* then *I can recreate myself.* I can become the person I want to be. If I had not created myself, I would also have no control over who I am in the future.

3. **I am responsible for myself.** Since I created myself, I am responsible for who I am. I am responsible for my beliefs because I chose to believe them, even if they later turn out to be wrong. I am responsible for my emotions and the impact they have on my behavior. I am responsible for the outcomes of my decisions and actions, whether they are positive or negative. As a leader, I am responsible for the environment I create.

This next point is extremely important: **If you are responsible for yourself, and everyone else is responsible for him or herself, then you are not responsible <u>for anyone</u> other than yourself.**

I had to think about this one for quite a while. My first thought was: "*But surely I am responsible for my children? As an employer, am I not responsible for my employees?*" Then I realized that I could not be responsible <u>for</u> them because I cannot control them. They have their own free will, can make their own decisions, and do whatever they want to do. If, for example, my son were to break the law, he will be held responsible, as he should be.

I am, however, responsible <u>to</u> them. I am responsible <u>to</u> my children to be the best parent I can be, to help them grow up to be the best they can be, and to be responsible for themselves. As the leader of our business, I am responsible <u>to</u> our employees: to create a respectful, trusting work environment so they enjoy coming to work, to create opportunities for them to use their talents and skills in ways that contribute to our organization's *purpose* and *vision*, to operate the business in alignment with our *core values*, and to ensure the business is financially successful and that employees are fairly compensated.

I have many responsibilities, but I must not take responsibility away from others. It robs them of their personal power and ultimately, if they allow me to continue to do it, of their self-esteem and dignity. Far too many organizations are taking responsibility <u>for</u> their employees, giving them no *choice* or *freedom* to use their talents, and then wondering why they are not *accountable*.

4. **The past does not control me.** What happened in the past does not have to control what you do in the future. Have you ever wondered what life would be like if only you had taken up that opportunity you had a few years ago? Or if you had pursued your dream when you left school rather than following your parents' choice for your college education? Regret something? Get over it! Living in the past is a sure way of making yourself unhappy with your future as well.

If what you've done in the past hasn't worked for you, if it still isn't working for you, change what you are doing. You owe it to yourself and everyone else you are responsible to. If you have a habit that you think is just the way you are, like losing your cool with people and yelling at them, understand that you created yourself to be like that. It does not need to control you any longer. If *you have created yourself* and *you are responsible for yourself*, you can change your habits. Since the past does not control you, you can create the future you want.

5. **There is nothing to be afraid of.** Does your mind immediately come up with exceptions to this? Public speaking, I've heard, is a greater fear for some people than the fear of death, heights, or spiders. This was once true for me. In a previous career as a salesperson, I was invited to a breakfast meeting for salespeople called the SWAP Club. Before you get any other ideas, it stood for: Salespersons With A Purpose. My friend didn't tell me that, at the meeting, I would have to stand up and introduce myself, say what I sold, and then give a *thought for the day*. I was petrified. I was in a room of fifty strangers, all of whom looked far more successful than I, and my brain was so fogged up by the panic I was feeling that I could not think of a worthwhile thought to share. My friend bailed me out by writing down a thought I could use, but when I stood up to speak, all that came out was a squeak. Paralysis strikes again!

I felt like a fool and thought I would never go back. I could not believe how afraid I was. Well, on further reflection, I began to think that maybe it would be good for me to go back and learn to overcome the fear. So I did, and yes, after a few weeks, I was speaking in a normal voice instead of a squeak. I was still nervous, but I was not afraid. Within a few months, the club member responsible for finding a speaker each week decided to step down, so I volunteered for the position. It meant I had to introduce and thank the speaker each week—by then I wanted to stretch myself even further. A year later, I was elected President of the club and was leading all the meetings.

Fear is what holds people back from achieving their potential. Fear is what holds managers back from trusting people to do the right thing. Fear of making mistakes holds many people back from making decisions or trying out new ways of doing things. Fear of other people making mistakes leads to micromanaging and bureaucracy and kills innovation and creativity. Much of what I've suggested you do throughout this book involves you taking a risk. It is risky to attempt new behaviors and to open yourself up to being more vulnerable. There is a risk to trusting people. Unfortunately, some will let you down. You need to learn to trust yourself to be able to deal with whatever happens. Dealing with fear is never easy, but we ultimately find that what once frightened us, when confronted, usually makes us laugh at ourselves a little when we realize exactly what we were afraid of, which was fear itself. Having fears is human. Overcoming these fears is a triumph to your spirit and a tribute to what you can achieve.

When I realized that I could deal with the embarrassment of making a mistake in front of other people, the fear of speaking in public decreased significantly. What fears hold you back? The fear you have about taking a risk may not be as much about what you have to do as it is about being able to deal with the change or how other people may react to you. You can function when you are experiencing fear, just like I did at the breakfast meeting. I was fearful of speaking in front of those people every week, but I still got up and did it. You can too. Just have faith in yourself.

6. **The answers are within me.** As you were reading through the various concepts and ideas in this book, I am sure there were many times you said to yourself, "*Yes, that makes sense to me.*" You intuitively knew a lot of this, if not in so many words. You knew that most people are basically good, honest, decent folks who want to make a difference in some way. You also knew you could not achieve very much as a leader without them.

I hope that what I've been able to share with you will help you be the leader you want to be and achieve the results you deserve. Listen to your intuition—*the answers are within you!* Enjoy the journey.

APPENDIX

HOW **PASSIONATE** ARE **YOU?**

How passionate are you in your current work environment? As mentioned in the introduction to this book, there are five levels of personal needs employees have that must be satisfied for employees to feel passionate about their work and their organization.

The more passionate employees are, the larger the payoff is to the organization. The diagram below shows the complete **Passion Pyramid**™, with the five levels of employee needs, the five *leadership skills* needed to satisfy these needs, and the *organizational payoff* when these needs are met.

The Passion Pyramid ™
© 2008 Integro Leadership Institute

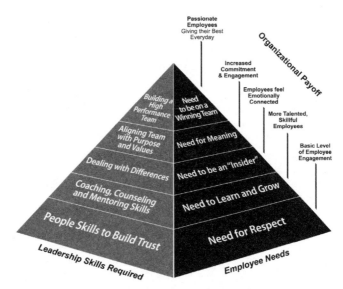

Figure out your Passion Index online at www.engagementisnotenough.com

The Passion Index

The following statements are designed to measure your attitudes towards your organization, the people you work with, and the job you perform. There are two aspects of these needs that determine how passionate you will be:

1. How important each need is to you personally.
2. Your perception of the performance of your organization, manager, or team in satisfying the need.

Your passion will be highest when the needs that are most important to you are being fully satisfied by your organization, manager, or team.

Directions:

- Answer each question by circling the number under what you feel is most accurate; your first response is usually the most accurate.
- When you have finished Section I, add up the numbers circled to get your Personal Needs score.
- When you have finished Section II, again total the numbers circled to get your Workplace Performance score.
- Then measure the gap by subtracting your Workplace Performance score **from** your Personal Needs score. Finally, subtract your gap score from 100 to determine your Passion Index. The higher your score, the more passionate you are about your work.

SECTION I
Your Personal Needs
How important are the following needs to you personally?

The Need to Be Respected
1. My immediate manager or supervisor trusts me and treats me with respect.

How important is this to you personally?

1	2	3	4	5	6	7	8	9	10

Not Important   *Very Important*

2. My organization's policies and practices regarding compensation, work/life balance, and valuing diversity demonstrate respect for all employees.

How important is this to you personally?

1	2	3	4	5	6	7	8	9	10

Not Important   *Very Important*

The Need to Learn and Grow
3. I have the opportunity to increase my knowledge and develop new skills in my job.

How important is this to you personally?

1	2	3	4	5	6	7	8	9	10

Not Important   *Very Important*

4. My organization invests in developing the potential of all employees.

How important is this to you personally?

1	2	3	4	5	6	7	8	9	10

Not Important   *Very Important*

The Need to Be an Insider
5. My immediate manager or supervisor values my contribution and cares about my well-being.

How important is this to you personally?

1	2	3	4	5	6	7	8	9	10

Not Important   *Very Important*

6. My organization is open with employees about information and organizational performance to help us understand the decisions that are being made.

How important is this to you personally?

1   2   3   4   5   6   7   8   9   10
Not Important   *Very Important*

The Need for Meaning
7. The mission or purpose of my organization makes me feel proud to work here.

How important is this to you personally?

1   2   3   4   5   6   7   8   9   10
Not Important   *Very Important*

8. The work I do is meaningful because it helps my organization fulfill our mission.

How important is this to you personally?

1   2   3   4   5   6   7   8   9   10
Not Important   *Very Important*

The Need to Be Part of a Winning Team
9. My team is making a significant contribution to our organization.

How important is this to you personally?

1   2   3   4   5   6   7   8   9   10
Not Important   *Very Important*

10. My team is focused on continually improving our performance.

How important is this to you personally?

1   2   3   4   5   6   7   8   9   10
Not Important   *Very Important*

Please add up your circled numbers to get your *Personal Needs* score:

_____

SECTION II
Your perception of the performance of your organization, manager, or team in satisfying these needs

How would you rate the performance of your organization, manager, or team in satisfying the following needs?

The Need to Be Respected

1. My immediate manager or supervisor trusts me and treats me with respect.

How would you rate your manager's performance in satisfying this need?

1	2	3	4	5	6	7	8	9	10

Very Poor   *Excellent*

2. My organization's policies and practices regarding compensation, work/life balance, and valuing diversity demonstrate respect for all employees.

How would you rate your organization's performance in satisfying this need?

1	2	3	4	5	6	7	8	9	10

Very Poor   *Excellent*

The Need to Learn and Grow

3. I have the opportunity to increase my knowledge and develop new skills in my job.

How would you rate your organization's performance in satisfying this need?

1	2	3	4	5	6	7	8	9	10

Very Poor   *Excellent*

4. My organization invests in developing the potential of all employees.

How would you rate your organization's performance in satisfying this need?

1	2	3	4	5	6	7	8	9	10

Very Poor   *Excellent*

The Need to Be an Insider

5. My immediate manager or supervisor values my contribution and cares about my well-being. How would you rate your manager's performance in satisfying this need?

1	2	3	4	5	6	7	8	9	10

Very Poor   *Excellent*

6.   My organization is open with employees about information and organizational performance to help us understand the decisions that are being made.

How would you rate your organization's performance in satisfying this need?

1	2	3	4	5	6	7	8	9	10
Very Poor									*Excellent*

The Need for Meaning

7. The mission or purpose of my organization makes me feel proud to work here.

How would you rate your organization's performance in satisfying this need?

1	2	3	4	5	6	7	8	9	10
Very Poor									*Excellent*

8. The work I do is meaningful because it helps my organization fulfill our mission.

How would you rate your organization's performance in satisfying this need?

1	2	3	4	5	6	7	8	9	10
Very Poor									*Excellent*

The Need to Be Part of a Winning Team

9. The team I work for is making a significant contribution to our organization.

How would you rate your team's performance in satisfying this need?

1	2	3	4	5	6	7	8	9	10
Very Poor									*Excellent*

10. My team is focused on continually improving our performance.

How would you rate your team's performance in satisfying this need?

1	2	3	4	5	6	7	8	9	10
Very Poor									*Excellent*

Please add up your circled numbers to get your *Workplace Performance* score:

_____

Identifying your Passion Index

Measure the gap by subtracting your *Workplace Performance* score
_____ *from* your *Personal Needs* score _____ to determine your gap score _____.
Subtract your gap score from 100 to get your **Passion Index** score:
_____.

The *higher* your **Passion Index** score is, the *more passionate* you are
about your work and your workplace.

INTERPRETING YOUR PASSION INDEX SCORE

Above Average Scores

86 to 100: Scores in this range indicate that you are passionate about your work and your work environment. Your manager cares about you as a person, not just as a means to achieve results, and your organization's leaders demonstrate through words and deeds that their people are their most valuable asset. The trust level in your organization is high.

Average Scores

75 to 85: Scores in this range indicate that your passion about your work and/or your work environment has declined. You may still feel passionate about your work, but have concerns that your manager and the organization do not value employees as much as they say they do. Trust is diminished. Significant improvement in performance could be achieved if more attention were paid to employees' expectations and needs and to building trust.

Below Average Scores

61 to 74: Scores in this range indicate that any passion you feel at work is likely to be restricted to some aspects of your job or the people you work with, rather than the organization you work for. These needs are important to you, and yet your manager and/or your organization's senior leaders don't realize it or don't care. The trust level is low, but not beyond repair if corrective actions were taken now. You may be feeling disillusioned and thinking about looking for another job.

Dangerously Low Scores

60 and lower: If you have scored in this range, the *fire within* has been extinguished and you are most likely actively looking for another job. The trust level is so low that even if your manager and organization's leaders woke up and committed to meeting employees' needs and expectations, it may be too late to win you back.

NOTES

Introduction

1. Curt Coffman and Gabriel Gonzalez-Molina, Ph.D., *Follow this Path: How the World's Greatest Organizations Drive Growth by Unleashing Human Potential* (Warner Business Books, 2002) 137.

2. Curt Coffman and Gabriel Gonzalez-Molina, Ph.D., *Follow this Path: How the World's Greatest Organizations Drive Growth by Unleashing Human Potential* (Warner Business Books, 2002) 136.

3. Marcus Buckingham and Donald O. Clifton, Ph.D., *Now, Discover Your Strengths* (The Free Press, 2001).

4. Daniel Goleman, Richard Boyatzis and Annie McKee, *Primal Leadership: Realizing the Power of Emotional Intelligence* (Harvard Business School Press, 2002).

5. Jim Collins, *Good to Great: Why Some Companies Make the Leap ... and Other's Don't* (Harper Business, 2001).

Chapter 2

6. Martin E.P. Seligman, Ph.D., *Learned Optimism: How to Change Your Mind and Your Life* (Free Press, re-issue 1998).

Chapter 4

7. Author correspondence with Leigh Branham, author of *The 7 Hidden Reasons Employees Leave.*

Chapter 5

8. Daniel Goleman, *Working with Emotional Intelligence* (Bloomsbury Publishing Plc., January 1, 1999).

9. Daniel Goleman, Richard Boyatzis and Annie McKee, *Primal Leadership: Realizing the Power of Emotional Intelligence* (Harvard Business School Press, 2002).

Chapter 7

10. James C. Collins and Jerry I. Porras, *Built to Last: Successful Habits of Visionary Companies* (Century Ltd., 1994) 8.

11. Jeffrey Pfeffer and Charles A. O'Reilly III, *Hidden Value: How Great Companies Achieve Extraordinary Results with Ordinary People* (Harvard Business School Press, 2000) 233.

12. Jim Collins, *Good to Great and the Social Sectors* (© Jim Collins 2005) 15.

13. Jeffrey Pfeffer and Charles A. O'Reilly III, *Hidden Value: How Great Companies Achieve Extraordinary Results with Ordinary People* (Harvard Business School Press, 2000) 233 to 243.

Chapter 10

14. Thomas A. Harris, M.D., *I'm OK - You're OK* (Arrow Books, 1995).

15. Thomas A. Harris, M.D., *I'm OK - You're OK* (Arrow Books, 1995) 36 to 41.

Chapter 11

16. James C. Collins and Jerry I. Porras, *Built to Last: Successful Habits of Visionary Companies* (Century Ltd., 1994) 73.

17. James C. Collins and Jerry I. Porras, *Built to Last: Successful Habits of Visionary Companies* (Century Ltd., 1994) 78.

18. James C. Collins and Jerry I. Porras, *Built to Last: Successful Habits of Visionary Companies* (Century Ltd., 1994) 69.

19. James C. Collins and Jerry I. Porras, *Built to Last: Successful Habits of Visionary Companies* (Century Ltd., 1994) 77.

20. Kenneth W. Thomas, *Intrinsic Motivation at Work: Building Energy & Commitment* (Berrett Koehler, 2000).

21. Kenneth W. Thomas, *Intrinsic Motivation at Work*: *Building Energy & Commitment* (Berrett Koehler, 2000).

Chapter 12

22. Jon R. Katzenbach and Douglas K. Smith, *The Wisdom of Teams: Creating the High-Performance Organization* (Collins Business Essentials, 1999).

23. Arlen Leholm and Raymond Vlasin, *Increasing the Odds for High-Performance Teams: Lessons Learned* (Michigan State University Press, 2006).

24. Arlen Leholm and Raymond Vlasin, *Increasing the Odds for High-Performance Teams: Lessons Learned* (Michigan State University Press, 2006).

25. Jim Collins, *Good to Great and the Social Sectors* (© Jim Collins 2005).

RECOMMENDED RESOURCES

The following resources have been developed by Integro Leadership Institute to help organizations create a work environment where employees want to, and can, perform at their best every day. **For more information on any of the following resources, go to www.engagementisnotenough.com.**

Leadership Development Process ™
Developing the leadership skills needed to ignite the passion in all employees takes time and disciplined application. This five-step process equips leaders with the skills and the tools they need (as outlined in this book) to apply what they are learning at each step with their teams back at work. Each step in the process focuses leaders on both the *employee needs* and the *organizational payoff* as they work their way up the **Passion Pyramid**™.

Senior Team Alignment Process ™
Creating a work environment based on trust and personal responsibility must start at the top of the organization. This three-step process ensures that <u>all</u> members of the senior team are *on the bus* and committed to following through on their responsibility to the mission, vision, and values of the organization. The **Team Alignment Questionnaire**™ is used to measure the *trust level* and alignment on *purpose, vision,* and *values* in the senior team, before and after, so that progress can be measured.

Team Development Process ™
This three-step process helps intact teams or project teams at any level of the organization to build a high level of trust, eliminate unproductive conflict, and get into alignment on the team's purpose, values, vision, and goals. Through the use of assessment tools such as the **Team Alignment Questionnaire**™ and **Team Member Rating**™, this process significantly increases the odds of becoming a *high-performance team.*

Strategic Alignment Survey ™
This survey measures four key areas that have an impact on employee alignment and engagement, and provides feedback by division, business unit, location, and work teams across the organization. The four sections of this report are:

- **Section I – Kinds of People** measures whether employees are perceived to be *responsible, rebellious* or *compliant.*
- **Section II – Group Trust-Level Report** measures the degree to which employees practice *trust-building behaviors.*
- **Section III – Values That Build Trust** measures the organization's performance in operating by these critical values.
- **Section IV – Group Alignment Report** measures the degree to which employees are *aligned* with the organization's *purpose, values, vision,* and *goals.*

Team Alignment Questionnaire™

This team assessment tool has been used by Integro's clients for over twenty-five years to identify the key areas that determine team effectiveness. It also provides a benchmark for our **Senior Team Alignment Process™** and **Team Development Process™** so that we can measure increased team effectiveness as the process evolves. The two dimensions measured by the report are:

- **Team Alignment** measures the level of clarity and agreement there is in the team on their *purpose, values, vision, goals, procedures,* and *roles.*
- **Team Trust Level** measures each team member's perception of the *level of trust* there is in the team.

Leadership Development Assessment™

This 360 degree assessment tool measures twenty-six competencies that managers need to create an environment where their team members will perform at the top of their game. There is a strong emphasis on *emotional intelligence* competencies, especially those that are necessary for *building trust.*

Team Member Rating™

This 360 degree assessment tool is used within an intact team to identify team members' perceptions of each other's contribution to the team in three areas:

- **Climate:** contribution to the trust level in the team
- **Process:** contribution to the way the team communicates and works together
- **Task:** contribution to the results the team achieves

Executive Coaching

Keith Ayers is available to provide executive coaching to help business leaders apply the principles in this book to improve their own leadership skills and increase employee passion. For more information, go to www.engagementisnotenough.

205

com, enter the access code on the last page of the book, and click on "executive coaching."

Speaking Engagements

A specialist in leadership development, organizational culture, and employee engagement, Keith Ayers has been working with executive teams for almost three decades. Keith has established his reputation as an innovative and impactful speaker and is equally effective addressing large or small groups. His approach is not overpowering and his knowledge and experience command respect. To have Keith appear live at your next event, go to www.engagementisnotenough.com, enter the access code on the last page of the book, and click on "speaking engagements."

DiSC® Classic

With thirty years of proven reliability and over 40 million users, Inscape's **DiSC Classic** remains the most trusted learning instrument in the industry. It is used worldwide in dozens of training and coaching applications, including organizational development and performance improvement. Designed to complement and supplement existing training programs, **DiSC Classic** can help improve communication, ease frustration and conflict, and develop effective managers and teams.

DiSC® Indra® – In-Depth Relationship Assessment

DiSC Indra's innovative model brings **DiSC** learning and understanding to the next level—that of the relationship itself. It maps and measures the relationships of people, providing individuals and groups with feedback concerning the interrelatedness of different **DiSC** styles. **DiSC Indra** is designed to highlight areas of compatibility and incompatibility, pinpointing individuals' differences and providing insight about how to work together more effectively.

Work Expectations Profile

In a typical employment situation, certain expectations, such as salary, hours, and job duties, are clearly understood by both employer and employee. Other expectations, however, are so intimately linked to an individual's concept of work that they often go unspoken or unacknowledged. The **Work Expectations Profile** helps people explore ten often unspoken work expectations that affect today's employment relationships and employee engagement.

*Personal Listening Profile**

It is estimated that people screen out or misunderstand the intended meaning or purpose of a message in over 70 percent of communications, making listening the biggest contributing factor to miscommunication. The **Personal Listening Profile*** helps individuals identify which of the five listening approaches they use to process, organize, store, and retrieve information, and through that awareness, increase their listening adaptability.

Team Dimensions Profile

Successful team members do not do the same thing at the same time. They do the right thing at the right time. The **Team Dimensions Profile** helps individuals work from their strengths by identifying their most natural team role, while giving them added appreciation for the contributions of others. The added bonus in the **Team Dimensions Profile** is that these natural team roles, when effectively combined, provide the team with a process to follow that increases team effectiveness by capitalizing on the leadership strengths of each team member.

*Discovering Diversity Profile**

As the dramatic shift to a highly diverse workplace continues, organizations know they must help employees understand, accept, and capitalize on differences. They know the cultural backgrounds and experiences of diverse employees and customers can enrich the organization, making it more innovative and globally competitive. The **Discovering Diversity Profile** helps organizations meet diversity challenges through a four-step process of Knowledge, Understanding, Acceptance, and Behavioral Skills.

Go to www.engagementisnotenough.com